Railway World Annual

CAMBRIAN COAST
EXPRESS
75033

Railway World Annual 1973

Edited by
ALAN WILLIAMS

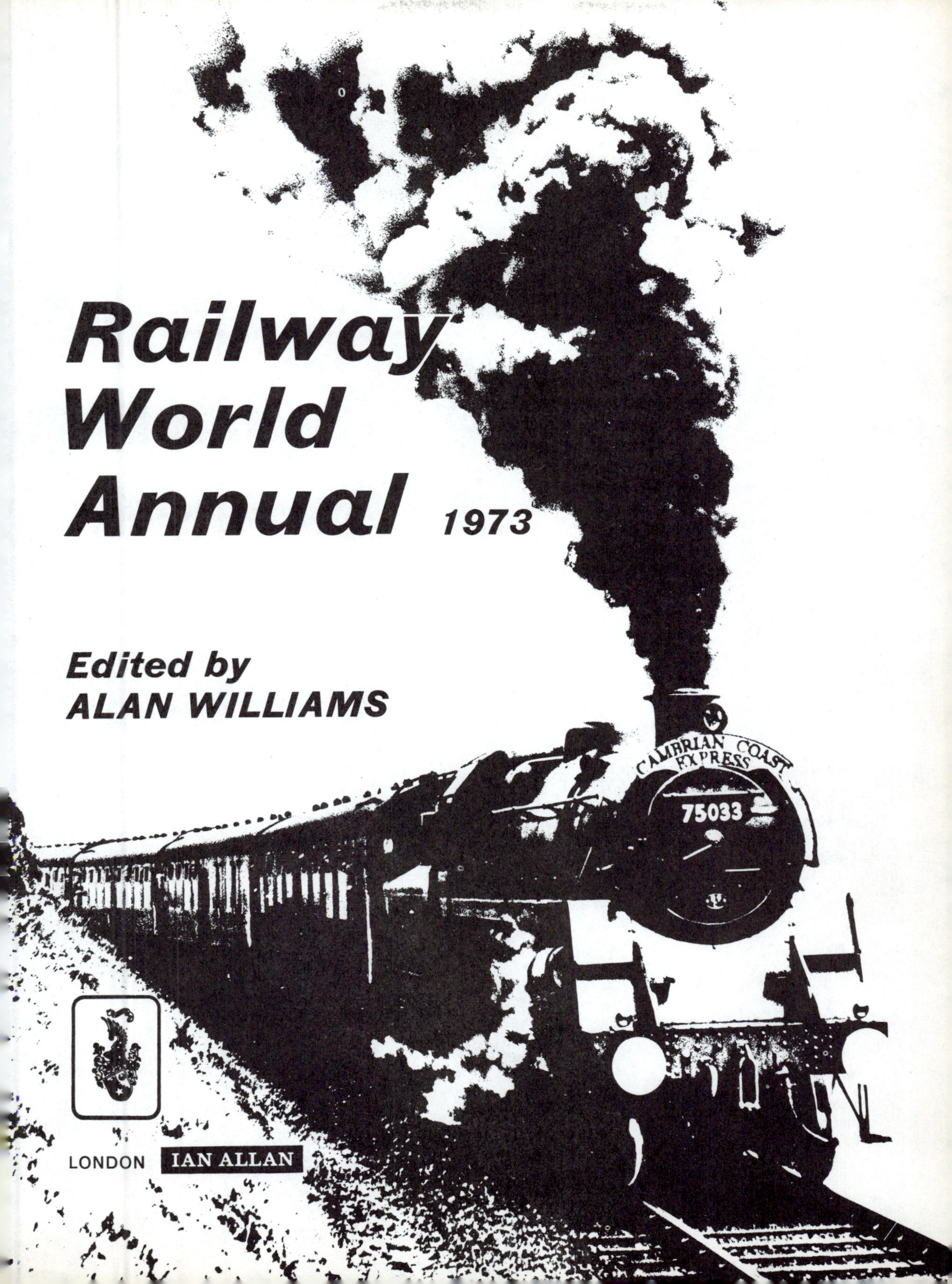

LONDON IAN ALLAN

First published 1972

SBN 7110 0377 7

Published by Ian Allan Ltd., Shepperton, Surrey and printed in the United Kingdom by A. Wheaton & Co., Exeter

Contents

Front cover: Preserved GW 9000 class 'Dukedog' 4-4-0 No 3217 *Earl of Berkeley* climbs away from Sheffield Park towards Horsted Keynes with an afternoon train on the Bluebell Railway *[John H. Bird*

Title page: BR standard class 4 4-6-0 No 75033 attacks the 1 in 52 of Talerddig Bank with the last London-bound 'Cambrian Coast Express' on March 4, 1967. *[Paul Claxton*

Fifty Years On

Fifty years ago the railways of Britain, having suffered the ravages of the Great War, were poised, somewhat unwillingly for the most part, on the edge of a giant step forward – Grouping. From the myriad of small, mostly struggling minor companies there emerged the 'Big Four'. The Government of the day had retreated from Nationalisation for the time being. But it was only a matter of time: 25 years and another World War later, there was no alternative, and the Big Four became one under British Railways. In Railway World Annual 1973, we look back at these last fifty years on Britain's Railways, 25 of them under the Big Four of Grouping, and as many years again under British Railways. We look at the squabbles that surrounded the choice of names for the Big Four, at the various pressures that were brought to bear on railway managements in the steam versus diesel versus electric battles, and how two World Wars, an intervening depression and a subsequent loss of faith affected the fortunes of both electric traction and railway carriage design.

During the period, the rural railway line has almost disappeared, and in some cases photographs are now almost all that remains. We look in particular at the Southern lines west of Exeter, where savage cuts have been made in the past decade, and at the Highland lines north of Inverness and the Cambrian lines of West Wales, where further pruning is threatened. There is a sad photo-feature on the rusting hulks of Barry scrapyard, although even here all is not completely lost; several locomotives, having stood condemned for several years, have been rescued, renovated and put to work on preserved lines.

In lighter vein, there are articles on railway operation from the railwayman's point of view, and a diary of the trials of railway enthusiasm in the Soviet Union. Then there is a short piece about the only remaining standard gauge railway on the Channel Islands, in Alderney, and as a change from the little railways of Wales a look at the little railways of England.

The railways of Britain have changed almost beyond recognition in the past 50 years, and show every sign of continuing to do so in the forseeable future. Here then is a record of just some of the many events, some important, some trivial, that have contributed to this massive change. I hope you will like it.

Alan Williams

Naming the 1923 'Big Four'

B. G. WILSON

When war broke out in August 1914 the Government took control of the railways of the United Kingdom, exercising power through a committee of general managers of the leading companies. In 1919 it set up the Ministry of Transport, whose first major task was to plan the future organisation of the railways, which were to remain in Government hands for another two years.

The first proposal, a nationalisation plan, stirred up such opposition that a compromise was evolved. By the Railways Act of 1921 the government decreed that all the major and all save the smallest of the minor railways of England, Scotland and Wales should be formed into four large groups, each with one or more 'constituent companies' absorbing a number of subsidiaries.

The groupings were worked out on a company basis, treating England, Scotland and Wales as one. The idea of a separate group for Scotland was soon ruled out in view of doubts whether it could pay its way in the changed economic climate of the early 1920s, with wages and prices far above pre-war levels. There was no attempt to regionalise by tidying up and transferring penetrating lines, though the new formations made such surgery less painful when State ownership finally came after the second world war.

Early in the railway age, Parliament had countenanced mergers such as those that had produced giants like the Midland in 1844 and the London & North Western in 1846. But fear of the rise of powerful monopolies made it subsequently concur in, if not indeed encourage, the creation and perpetuation of rivalries and competition. As George Dow writes in *Great Central*, 'Railway amalgamation had been fostered and then condemned; wildcat competitive schemes for railways had been sanctioned and the victims then afforded protection.' For example, a proposed merger of the Midland and Glasgow & South Western railways in the 1860s met not only the expected hostility of the London & North Western and Caledonian, partners in

Gresley class A1 Pacific No 1476 shortly after Grouping sporting the first LNER livery, including the initials 'L&NER' and the number on its tender.

the West Coast route to Scotland, but also that of the House of Lords, which was persuaded of the bad faith of the Derby board over the projected Settle–Carlisle line. As late as 1908 the Great Central, Great Northern and North Eastern produced a sensible plan for a working union. It got as far as a second reading, but had to be withdrawn because of the hostility it provoked. On the other hand, the Midland's smart take-over of the little London Tilbury & Southend in 1912 was blessed by Westminster, subject to guarantees for the Great Eastern and Great Northern. It is little wonder that, having been so often rebuffed by Parliament when they sought to merge or work more closely together, the railways now resented the shot-gun marriages the new Bill proposed to force on them.

The problems that grouping posed have nowhere been better summarised than in Cecil J. Allen's *The London & North Eastern Railway*, a fascinating account of the birth and life of the second biggest of the new grouped companies that came into being on January 1, 1923. So complex was the administrative and financial work that the problem of selecting names for the new giants might seem to have been a minor consideration. But it nevertheless gave the managements of two of the four groups some headaches and it produced a crop of suggestions, mostly unofficial, that ranged from the practical to the fanciful.

The 'Western' group was spared most of the anxieties of the others, nomenclature included, for the Act laid down that 'the amalgamation scheme shall provide for constituting the Great Western Railway Company the amalgamated company' of that group as it was so much larger and more important than all others affected. So the 'Great Western' was to live on for another 25 years as a still greater Great Western.

The south and south-east of England were served by the London & South Western, London Brighton & South Coast and South Eastern & Chatham railways, the last-named a hard-won working union of two companies which by 1899 had grown weary of 40 years of strife which Parliament had abetted. The merger of these three was not easily accomplished, even though the group was the smallest of the four. But largely thanks to Sir Herbert Walker, who as its general manager repeated his success as chairman of the wartime Railway Executive, it was to turn out well.

The 'Southern' group had little trouble over a name. Apparently there was wide agreement on the excellent choice of 'Southern Railway Company', which the *Railway Gazette* considered 'admirably terse'. 'Great Southern' strikes one as being the only good and concise alternative, with historical sanction, too, as it had been a likely choice for a union of the southern lines proposed many years before.

For the two largest of the 'Big Four' the choice of a suitably descriptive but not too cumbersome title was much trickier. The 'North Western, Midland and Scottish Group' of the Act included two English giants of like stature, the London & North Western and the Midland. Each had its trunk route right from London to the Border, each had lines in Wales and dense networks in the English industrial districts. The *Railway Gazette* favoured 'Midland & North Western', though this would have paid scant regard to the three not inconsiderable Scottish elements of the group: the Caledonian, Glasgow & South Western and Highland. A strong official candidate almost to the last was 'London Midland & Northern' but on November 24, 1922, almost the eleventh hour, the *Railway Gazette* learned that the final choice was 'London Midland & Scottish', a sonorous and descriptive title, if rather a mouthful, and one that recalled the frustrated St. Pancras–St Enoch union of the 1860s. The Railway Amalgamation Tribunal was not too keen on 'London Midland & Scottish' but finally agreed to let it stand.

For the Eastern Group the difficulty of settling on a suitable name was even more acute. The four English partners, North Eastern, Great Northern, Great Central and Great Eastern, were on more or less equal terms, though the North Eastern with its monopoly was the most prosperous. Obviously a title that would do justice to all four and yet not neglect the two Scottish partners, the North British – which served the West as well as the East Coast – and the Great North of Scotland, would take some finding. Matters might have been simplified had the Great Central become part of a 'Greater Midland' group, a notion favoured by the *Railway Gazette* in early 1922.

The November 24, 1922 issue of that journal reported Lord Knaresborough, chairman of the North Eastern, as saying, at a special meeting to approve terms of the merger, that after considering such suggestions as 'Great North', 'East Coast', 'Great North Eastern', 'Eastern' and 'East British' they had concluded that 'London & North Eastern' would suit them best. Rather partisanly he went on: 'North Eastern' designated the 'outstanding feature of the undertaking' and perpetuated the name of the largest and most important company in the group. The inclusion of 'London' would remind them that they of the North Eastern would 'no longer enjoy the advantages or share the disadvantages of being a provincial company.'

The *Railway Gazette* considered the name 'most happy', but then it had suggested it two years before when advocating an alternative to the grouping scheme, even though that article did not consider the inclusion of the Great Eastern and admitted only parts of the Great Central and North British.

It may be interesting to list some of the unofficial suggestions made in 1922 by correspondents to the *Railway Gazette*. For convenience they are listed under the name each group finally adopted.

Southern

South Eastern	London & Four Southern
London & South	Southern Lines
London & Southern	Great Southern & Eastern
South Anglian	
Southern Counties	

London Midland & Scottish

London & West Britain	Midland, Western & Northern
Mid-Western & Caledonian	North Mid Railways
Midland & North Western	Midland & West Northern
West Coast Joint Railways	Midland, West Northern & Highland
British North Western	
Midland	
Central	
North Western	

London & North Eastern

London & East Britain	Eastern Joint Railways
British Eastern	York & Joint Eastern Railways
Eastern	Central & East Northern
Eastern Railways	
Northern, Central & Eastern	Central, East Northern & West Highland
Great Northern & Eastern	

Some correspondents had to be reminded that the name Great Western Railway Company was fixed by the Act, a fact that would rule out such otherwise concise titles as 'Western.' It is noteworthy that most writers thought 'London' superfluous. One rightly observed that 'East Coast' would be inaccurate as both the Great Central and North British touched the West Coast and that 'West Coast' was equally to be rejected as the Midland – presumably by the Tilbury absorption – the Lancashire & Yorkshire (absorbed by the London & North Western in 1922) and Highland railways all touched the East Coast.

The correspondence did not become acrimonious, though E. A. Clear, Assistant General Manager of the Great Central, waxed sarcastic at the expense of a correspondent who had put forward British North Western, South Anglian and British Eastern or York & Joint Eastern. The idea of associating York was too parochial – the 'famous hamlet' of Billericay, he wrote, 'would be quite as convenient a headquarters for the Eastern Group as York!' An interesting aside now that, fifty years on, the successor of the LNER, the Eastern Region of BR, has its headquarters in York!

92125

The Appleby Job

F. HOPKINSON

The diversion of the slower West Coast route freights onto the Midland's Carlisle–Hellifield line at the end of 1967 resulted in the introduction of new locomen's diagrams, and as a result we at Lostock Hall lost our nightly freight job over the 'Long Drag'. This was the 19.35 Edge Hill – Carlisle, which we worked from Lostock Hall Junction to Appleby West, returning with the 01.20 Carlisle – Crewe. In any case, this working had by then become a diesel diagram in both directions, but any Lostock Hall man recounting his experiences on this duty will always refer to the days when we had steam locomotives rostered to it. A common conversation between firemen at the shed might go something like this:

1st man: 'Where've you been?'
2nd man: 'Appleby'
1st man: 'Did you stick?'

These few words tell quite a tale, for on heavily loaded trains we had to stop for a blow-up more than once, because of a poor engine, a bad rail, or an inexperienced fireman – and nowhere was a competent mate more necessary than on this road!

I was on this job during the first week of November 1967, the last week before Crewe South shed closed and a diesel locomotive was rostered regularly to the 01.20. The previous week a notice was received at our shed to the effect that a Type 2 diesel would be allocated to the 19.35, to utilise spare locomotives at Springs Branch before the introduction of full diesel diagrams at the new depot there. As I had just passed out for driving this type of diesel, I was looking forward to a trip with a Type 2 one way. Alas, the Edge Hill men who we were due to relieve that week had not been trained on Type 2s, so I had a steam loco-

Left: Two BR standard class 9Fs storm through Ribblehead with a heavy train of concrete-sleepered track on August 5, 1967.
[*Paul Riley*

Below: BR standard class 9F 2—10—0 No 92017 accelerates a northbound welded rail special through Appleby in May, 1967.
[*Derek Cross*

motive each night – much to the amusement of some of my mates!

I had a good mate that week – Harry Fowler, a pleasant lad and a natural comedian, just the right sort of company on a cold, dark overnight trip through the hills. And he was a good fireman. We started the week on the 19.35 with a Britannia, and with sister engine No 70051 on Tuesday, we had a rough time. On Wednesday, Thursday and Friday we had a Black 5 on the 19.35. We had a black'un each night on the 01.20. On the Thursday we had a fine night, two good engines, and the sort of trip I would have liked every night.

I booked on at our rostered time of 21.29 (a funny time to the layman, perhaps, but nothing out of the ordinary on the railway) and Control advised us that we had 44910 that night. The train was running late, so my mate and I went across to the Carriage Sidings signal box, on the back line, to await its arrival. Our scheduled departure time of 21.44 came and went, but still no sign – until 22.25, when Farington Junction box rang through to say that it was passing them. At half past ten our train crawled to a stand and we exchanged a brief word with the Liverpool crew. The driver said they had been sidetracked at St Helen's for 20 minutes or so and they had lost their path through Wigan. We had to get to Appleby for our meal break and nearly an hour of it had gone already! The fireman told my mate quickly '. . . the dampers are a bit dicky!' which in fact meant that they were closed tight. The fire was half-dead and we had 60 miles to go to Ais Gill Summit – mostly uphill – with '35 vehicles equal to 40'.

We took water at the Junction and with the aid of a stout piece of wood and a cob of coal as a lever, I managed to open the dampers while my mate put a good fire on. So much for the dicky dampers! Then at a quarter to eleven – one hour late – we were away. We didn't know then that the worst part of the night was over so far as the locomotives were

On a cold November morning in 1967 BR standard class 9F 2—10—0 No 92082 pounds up to Horton-in Ribblesdale with a freight for Carlisle.
[Dr. L. A. Nixon

Stanier class 8F 2—8—0 No 48399 hurries a fitted van train across Arten Gill Viaduct on its way up to Ais Gill Summit in October, 1966.
[*Dr. L. A. Nixon*

concerned, apart from the shovelling my mate had to do!

Engine No 44910 turned out to be a good steamer (now!) and we got going well over the hump to Blackburn and onto the Ribble Valley line to Hellifield. The weather was fine for November, a crisp starry night, with no moon to speak of, and our train was running very freely. About 12.15am the lights of Hellifield Station appeared away to our left. It always reminds me of a passenger train running through the night – just a line of lights across the fields. After a brief check at the distant to let a main line freight through, we rounded the long left-hand curve into Hellifield down loop and drew up to the water column. While my mate filled the tank I had a quick look round the engine. All was well and we were ready for away.

Once out of Hellifield we really got moving, right up to the 45mph allowed with our train, to give us a good run at the bank from Settle Junction. Around Settle Station the bank starts to pull you back, and with second valve and the wheel well forward we settled down to the steady slog up to Blea Moor. Apart from a brief acceleration as the bank eases near Horton, we maintained a steady 15–20mph all the way up. The engine was steaming well and the injectors gave us no trouble, so my mate had little bother keeping pressure well up and the water bobbing in the top nut of the gauge glass.

At night this road is as black as pitch. You don't realise how much reflected light comes from street or motor vehicle lights until you get right away from them, and up here at night there are hardly any lights at all! Even with the stars to help it was difficult to distinguish between the hilltops and the sky. The light of a lonely telephone kiosk near the line casts a glow which can be seen for miles, exaggerated by the surrounding darkness. And what of the signalmen at lonely spots like Selside, Blea Moor and Mallerstang. You begin to realise what a hardy race of men they must be, particularly in bad weather with only the wind for company and a stove and an oil lamp for comfort.

As we run up towards Horton-in-Ribblesdale, occasional flashes of grey in the gloom below show where the River Ribble rushes over the rocks on its way down to Preston and the sea. Then, amidst all the blackness, the lights of the limestone works at Horton appear before us like some large town in the middle of nowhere. Above Horton there is a different look about the sky. A line of cloud across it obscures the stars and sure enough it was raining at Ribblehead. What a God-forsaken spot this is! As we ran out onto the viaduct, the cross-wind hit us as it raced up the valley and, after being opened out just a little to counteract it, No 44910 still plugged away. To crown it all, as we ran into Blea Moor tunnel, the safety valves lifted – blowing off after almost 15 miles of 1 in 100. A quick look at the gauge glass showed the water well up in the boiler. What an engine! More important still, what a fireman!

Once into the damp murk of the tunnel the gradient eases and we can wind the wheel back. Speed rises rapidly for the run across the tops to Ais Gill. This must be one of the most impressive bits of railway anywhere in Britain with four tunnels and as many viaducts in the space of ten miles, not to mention Garsdale troughs where we drop the scoop to fill the tender for the run down to Carlisle. Night is not the time to see the grandeur of this road, but the 'feel' of it is with you all the time.

After Ais Gill we run down under easy steam and we can let the fire die down a bit to keep the engine from blowing off on the downhill run through Kirkby Stephen to Appleby. On arrival, we pulled up just south of the down platform and were relieved by a Kingmoor crew who had worked up on an earlier job. With a cheery word and nothing but praise for the engine we retired to the cabin alongside the large water tower on the up road for a brew and our 'scoff' – our name for the food we carry. It had been raining earlier at Appleby but it had cleared before we arrived, a good omen for the return trip. Coming up, we had regained nearly twenty minutes of the hour late start, not a bad effort with 35 equal to 40.

After our meal, I had a word with Carlisle

Below: Britannia Pacific No 70004 *William Shakespeare* eases a northbound coal train back onto the main line at Blea Moor, after a pause in the loop for water. It is June, 1967. [*B. Lister*

Right: Battling up the final yards to Ais Gill Summit comes Stanier class 5 4—6—0 No 44675 with the 05.30 Carlisle-Tinsley freight on April 27, 1967. [*Maurice Burns*

44675

Control on the phone to find out about our return train. We were getting 45349 with '36 equal to 40', and it was running to time. My mate had just stretched out on a form for a quick rest when a freight came clanking up to the column outside, and as ours was the only steam-hauled freight due in about that time, I nipped out to see what was what. I found 45253 with Holbeck men on the 01.00 Carlisle–Tinsley, normally a diesel job. You can imagine the long faces! Back in the cabin we had another ten minutes before a quick whistle told us that our train was drawing in. Skipton men brought it from Carlisle and, from Appleby, rode in the brake to Hellifield. We filled the tank and then were off home.

We ran quickly out of Appleby and I gave her some stick to take advantage of the short downhill to Ormside before settling down to the steady slog up to Ais Gill. This was another good engine, with good injectors, and again my mate did his stuff. Up through Kirkby Stephen we were doing a steady 20mph when we got a distant on ahead of us, and all the boards were on at Mallerstang. Those Holbeck men were not getting on too well with 45253 and hadn't yet cleared Ais Gill. However, as we drew slowly up to the peg, it came off and we started again at the worst part of the bank. Fortunately, the rain had cleared here as well and 45349 got hold of the train well to take us up past Ais Gill and across the top to Blea Moor. Here we got another yellow from the Tinsley, so I took it easily down the other side to let him get away from us. It was still raining and blowing at Ribblehead – no wonder they use it as a weather station!

After an uneventful run down the other side, I decided to take water at Settle as 45253 would almost certainly be using the column at Hellifield. I was proved right because, as we ran into the up platform at Hellifield, the Tinsley was standing in the up loop alongside the column, having taken water. Pausing briefly to drop the Skipton crew, we pulled across onto the Blackburn line. Our guard at Appleby had given me the loading as 36 equal to 46 (not 40) and this is over the limit allowed for a Black 5 up Wilpshire bank. I toyed with the idea of going it alone as we had a good strong engine, but stalling on the bank with an overloaded train means trouble (and I could not have proved what Carlisle Control had said on the phone) so I whistled up for the banker at Whalley. Unfortunately, the bank engine was up at Blackburn, so we had a forty minute wait while he finished whatever he was doing and followed a freight down to Whalley. The banker was one of our class 4 2–6–0s; after he had crossed over and buffered up we exchanged whistles and climbed quickly to Wilpshire where he dropped off. By this time dawn was breaking, and as we ran into Blackburn we could see the early morning traffic beginning to move. We waited in the loop for a passenger train to leave for Preston, then we were allowed out onto the main line for the final lap back to Lostock Hall Junction. We arrived back at 07.20, over an hour late, but this was not too bad, considering the delays we had suffered – and it was a tight schedule for a freight. We handed over to two more of our lads and then went home to bed.

Looking back at the Appleby job, you really had to work the trains; there was no room for playing about and some of our firemen took great pride in making a success of the job, hence the question I mentioned at the beginning. Even in the palmy days of steam, this job was still hard work, but with the run-down locomotives of 1967/8 it was often touch and go until you passed Ais Gill or Blea Moor. One day that week I remember we had 44878, a Kingmoor engine which never had a good reputation at our shed. By pure coincidence it came to Lostock Hall to eke out its last days after Kingmoor closed. It was still not much good and I longed for a 4910 or a 5349 when I got it on a job. This was a peculiar feature of steam locomotives – some always seemed to be inferior to the others of the same class, and this was one of them. Amongst Black 5's a bad 'un really made you remember. Without doubt, though, the most lasting impression of the Appleby job – quite apart from that in your pay packet on Friday – was that even with diesels, when you got on to the Midland, you were competing with nature.

Storming up to Kirkby Stephen with a southbound freight on November 2, 1967, comes the erstwhile *Royal Star*, Britannia class BR standard Pacific No 70028. [Derek Cross

Drifting across Ais Gill viaduct with a Carlisle-Skipton freight on November 2, 1967, is Stanier class 5 4—6—0 No 44857. [Derek Cross

Ninety Years of Electric Railways

ALAN WILLIAMS

Many railway enthusiasts tend to think of electric traction as some nasty new-fangled device intended to do away with steam engines. But it was as long ago as 1839, before many of today's main lines were even built, that the first successful electric locomotive was built. The brainchild of one Davidson, it was powered by a 40-cell iron/zinc battery and is reported to have achieved a speed of 4 mph on a line near Edinburgh. This diminutive machine obviously needed considerable development before it could match the performance of its steam-driven contemporaries, but even at this early stage steam railway engineers were suspicious of this potential rival, and it is said that a group of them contrived to wreck Davidson's locomotive.

These early steam protagonists clearly succeeded in suppressing further developments of any note, because it was well over forty years later, on August 3, 1883, that the first public electric railway in Britain was opened. The work of Magnus Volk, it was originally a 2ft gauge line running for about $\frac{1}{4}$ mile along the front at Brighton. The first trains took current from the running rails, but early the following year, the line was relaid to 2ft 8$\frac{1}{2}$in gauge and extended to a total length of 1$\frac{5}{8}$ miles. A third rail was provided to carry the 50V dc current to the cars. This was almost certainly the first use of the 'conductor rail' as we know it today.

Now, for the first time, electric traction began to be considered seriously for new suburban lines, and particularly the projected London underground lines. The City of London and Southwark Subway Co, later the City and South London Railway, was originally promoted in 1884 as a cable-operated tube line under the Thames from King William Street, in the City, to the Elephant and Castle. But before construction had advanced very far, it was decided to adopt electric traction. The first trial trains, using small four-wheeled locomotives, ran in the completed sections of tunnel in 1889. The line was electrified at 500V dc, with a centre third rail, return being through the running rails. Unlike modern systems, the third rail was not originally raised above the level of the running rails – in fact, it was a little below it – and to avoid the pick up shoes fouling the running rails at points and crossings, wooden ramps were provided.

Despite the austere nature of the original rolling stock – the well-nigh windowless and heavily upholstered carriages were soon christened 'padded cells' – the line was an immediate success. So much so, in fact, that at one stage the Company had to increase their fares during the morning and evening peak periods to discourage patronage at these times until station extensions and signalling improvements were completed.

Meanwhile, the Directors of the Liverpool Overhead Railway, which had been proposed in 1882 as a steam line, decided to opt for electric traction, and construction commenced in 1889. The main part of the line was opened for traffic in 1893; again the traction supply was 500V dc with a centre third conductor rail, although it was moved to the more conventional outside position in 1905. Here, for the first time, electric trains as opposed to locomotives were used. The first trains consisted of two motor coaches, arranged back-to-back, with control positions at the outer ends. Westinghouse air brakes were provided on both these and the City and South London trains, and this more powerful brake has been fitted, with minor modifications, to almost all electric locomotives and multiple-unit trains built in Britain since.

By 1895, electric traction had established itself beyond doubt as the most speedy and efficient form of transport for suburban lines, and it seemed that its adaptation to the requirements of long-distance main line work could be fairly readily accomplished. But the main line railway companies were not

The present era of 25kV ac overhead electrification began in 1955 with the proposal to electrify the LNWR main lines from Euston to Manchester and Liverpool. The first sections to be energised were between Crewe and Manchester and Crewe and Liverpool. Here, a decade later and now in British Rail blue livery, one of the first multiple-unit sets, AM4/1 unit No 006, heads for Liverpool on a semi-fast working.

[*British Rail*

Above: Trains pass at Children's Playground station on Volk's Electric Railway, Brighton. On this line, the offset centre-third conductor rail is still in use.
[*Anthony A. Vickers*

Left: One of the original City and South London Railway 0—4—0 electric locomotives stands in the hydraulic lift at Stockwell Depot. Note the original centre-third conductor rail on the track in the foreground.

Below: A three car train of un-rebuilt stock leaves St James Station for Dingle on the now-dismantled Liverpool Overhead Railway.
[*H. C. Casserley*

impressed, even for suburban work; they believed in the 'economy' of the well-tried steam engine, with its cheap, abundant fuel. At this time, manpower and its costs were not a problem. Why, then, should they want to spend large sums of money on non-prestigious suburban electrification schemes? But within a few years, the advent of the electric tramcar dramatically changed the situation; the inner suburban lines around London, Liverpool, Manchester and Newcastle, in particular, began to lose passengers to this new form of transport at an alarming rate.

The North Eastern Railway was the first of the major railway companies to realise that the tide could only be turned by the provision of an equally fast, clean and frequent electric railway service. Accordingly, in March 1904, almost seventy years ago, the NER introduced electric trains on the North Tyneside group of lines radiating east from Newcastle Central. Simultaneously, the Lancashire & Yorkshire Railway, which was facing similar troubles in the Liverpool area, introduced electric trains between Liverpool and Southport.

The little Mersey Railway, which provided access from Liverpool under the Mersey to the Wirral peninsular, had already converted its line from steam to electric throughout in 1903. Both the North Eastern and L&Y systems employed the outside third conductor rail, the former at 600V dc and the latter at 630V dc. The Mersey Railway, however, opted for the third and fourth rail system, with return via an insulated fourth rail between the tracks, rather than via the running rails, as on the other two lines. Here, the traction voltage was 650V dc. Considering the novelty of the systems and their equipment, all three lines ran remarkably well from the outset, providing further proof, if any were needed, of the reliability of electric traction in everyday intensive use. But still the railway companies ignored the large scale possibilities of electrification.

Perhaps because it had been slightly jolted by a proposal to build an entirely new rival electric line to Brighton in 1900, the London, Brighton & South Coast Railway alone among the larger companies began to consider seriously the possibilities of electrification. It, too, was now suffering seriously from electric tramway competition, but it began also to investigate the longer term possibilities of total electrification. One of the problems of medium voltage dc electrification is the large number of substations required. This is no problem in heavily-trafficked suburban areas, but becomes expensive when the system is applied to long distance main lines. The same problem does not arise with high voltage ac, and accordingly, with an eye to future electrification of its main lines to the coast, the Brighton opted for the initially more expensive 6600V ac overhead system. They were no doubt encouraged by the decision of the Midland Railway directors to electrify the Lancaster–Morecambe–Heysham section of their line on the same system. The Midland scheme came into operation in April 1908, while the Brighton, which ran into trouble with the erection of its overhead masts, began electric working on the South London line between Victoria and London Bridge in 1909.

Again, the electrification was an immediate success, with a gratifying increase in the number of passengers. In 1911 the 'Overhead Electric', as it was extensively advertised, was extended from Battersea Park, on the South London line, along the Brighton main line through Clapham Junction to Balham, and then via Streatham Hill and Crystal Palace to Selhurst. Although electric trains normally kept to the slow lines, the fast lines were also electrified through Clapham Junction to Balham. In the following year, the Peckham Rye-Tulse Hill- West Norwood Junction line, together with the spur from Tulse Hill to Leigham Junction, was opened to electric trains, and in 1913 work commenced on the electrification of the remainder of the LBSCR suburban lines, including the main line from Balham to what is now Coulsdon North via Streatham Common, Selhurst and East Croydon; from Selhurst to Sutton via West Croydon; and from Tulse Hill to Cheam via Streatham, Mitcham Junction and Sutton. Much work had been done and a considerable

Above: North Eastern Railway electric locomotive No 2 joins the main line near Manors with a freight from East Quay. For safety reasons, this steeply-graded branch and its associated quayside lines were electrified on the overhead system, and therefore electric locomotives Nos 1 and 2 were fitted with both pantographs and third-rail shoegear.

Left: A six-car train formed of two LSWR three-car 'nutcracker' units rounds the bend to East Putney on a Wimbledon-Waterloo via East Putney working. The centre fourth conductor rail installed here enabled District line trains from Putney Bridge to run over LSWR metals to Wimbledon.

Left: A three-car train of original L&Y wide-bodied stock heads for Liverpool on a stopping service from Southport. The trains had no contact with the centre fourth conductor rail which was installed here, as on some other electrified lines, to assist efficient return of the traction current.

amount of overhead equipment erected when War broke out in 1914 and the supply of further equipment from Germany abruptly ceased.

Meanwhile, some of the other companies were beginning, at last, to realise the potential of electric traction, at least as far as suburban work was concerned. Both the London and South Western and London and North Western Railways announced plans for electrification of their suburban lines, while the Lancashire & Yorkshire revealed its scheme for the first electrification in the Manchester area, from Manchester to Bury and Holcombe Brook. All three schemes employed the conductor rail system, but in different forms.

The first to open was the Bury–Holcombe Brook section of the Manchester–Bury scheme in 1913. This was originally electrified at 3500V dc, using the protected side contact third rail system of collection, rather than the more usual unprotected top contact system. Difficulty was encountered in maintaining insulation under certain weather conditions, and in 1916, when the Manchester-Bury section was opened, the voltage was reduced to 1200V dc throughout. The unusual side-contact form of collection was retained, however, and although new stock was introduced in 1959, remains in use today – the only example in Britain.

The first LNWR electric trains began to work between Willesden and Earls Court on May 1, 1914, and between Broad Street and Richmond, via Willesden and Hampstead Heath, in 1916. Meanwhile, from 1915, the London Electric Railway's Bakerloo tube trains had been running over LNWR metals between Queens Park and Willesden, and in 1917 this service was extended to Watford. Finally, in 1922, on completion of track alterations in the Primrose Hill area, LNWR electric trains commenced operation between Euston and Watford, and from Broad Street to Watford via Chalk Farm (now Primrose Hill). In that year also, the short branch from Watford High Street to Croxley Green was electrified.

The LSWR, having watched the suburban traffic on its Thames Valley suburban routes dwindle dramatically in the face of tramway competition for ten years, announced somewhat belatedly in early 1913 that it intended to electrify its entire Thames Valley suburban network. Following a visit to the United States by their Electrical Engineer, and encouraged by their Consulting Engineers, the South Western board decided to adopt the 600V dc outside third method of electrification, with running rail return. As if to make amends for their previous tardiness, work began quickly in July 1913, but the outbreak of war in the following year delayed progress.

Unlike the Brighton, however, the South Western was using British electrical contractors, so despite wartime conditions, it was decided to press on with the installation work so that in due course the surplus steam engines and staff could be released for war work. The first trains ran in October 1915 on the now-discontinued Waterloo–Wimbledon via East Putney service. The Kingston 'roundabout' and Shepperton lines were ready by December, but because of allegations from the Post Office of electrical interference with their equipment, electric services did not begin until the end of January 1916. The Hounslow loop was electrified in March, the Hampton Court branch in June, and the spur to Claygate in November. Figures published by the LSWR after the war showed that the number of passengers carried on the electrified lines more than doubled between 1915 and 1920.

Before passing on to the post-war period, mention must be made of the North Eastern Railway's historically important pilot main line electrification, from Newport, near Middlesbrough, to Shildon. Having been in the van of suburban railway electrification with their North Tyneside scheme in 1903, the North Eastern began to examine the possibilities of main line electrification. Mineral traffic on the North Eastern at this time was very high, and just prior to the War it was announced that the Shildon–Newport line, which carried very heavy mineral traffic, would be electrified at 1500V dc on the overhead system. Ten 1100hp Bo+Bo electric locomotives were designed and built by the

BURY
BOLTON STREET

10
10

Above: The driver of a train for Lancaster poses alongside his cab at Morecambe Promenade. The motor coach in the foreground is one of the original Midland Railway vehicles built for the opening of electrification in 1908. When the line was re-equipped as a proving ground for BR 25kV ac electrification in the early 1950s, this stock was scrapped and converted LNWR Siemens stock from the withdrawn Willesden-Earls Court service was introduced. [*W. Hubert Foster*

Above left: A five-car train of L&Y stock leaves Manchester Victoria Station for Bury. Although new BR standard stock has now been provided for this line, the protected side-contact third rail is still in use, the sole example in Britain. [*W. Hubert Foster*

Right: The motor coach of an LBSCR five-car unit built for the short-lived 1925 overhead ac extensions. After withdrawal in 1928, these vehicles were stripped of their electrical equipment and converted to freight bogie brake vans. [*H. C. Casserley*

Left: Strong American influence was evident in the design of the original Mersey Railway clerestory stock, a three-car train of which is seen here entering Birkenhead Central from Rock Ferry. When new BR-built stock was introduced in 1956, the line was converted to third rail throughout and the centre fourth conductor rail was removed. [*W. Hubert Foster*

Right: The compartment motor coach of an LBSCR three-car unit built in 1911 for the extension of the 'overhead electric' services to Crystal Palace. [*O. J. Morris*

NER to work the line. This was the first application of overhead high voltage dc, but apparently the line was a success, because the North Eastern announced its intention to electrify its main line between York and Newcastle, and in 1922 produced a 1800hp prototype high-speed electric locomotive, ominously, as it later transpired, numbered 13.

The Grouping in 1923 brought many problems, not the least of them being the incompatability of the many electrification systems now brought together under three of the new 'Big Four' companies. The new Southern Railway probably faced the greatest problem; the LSWR had bequeathed a completed 600V dc third rail system, the LBSCR an incomplete 6600V ac overhead system, and the SECR an as yet unstarted scheme for third and fourth rail electrification at 1500V dc. And as if to emphasise the need for a quick decision and rapid implementation, the Railway was being subjected to ferocious press criticism of the punctuality, frequency and cleanliness of its steam-worked services. The board lost no time, and set up a committee to examine the problem under the chairmanship of the Chief Operating Superintendent; this soon recommended the adoption of the South Western's 600V dc third rail system on the grounds of ease of installation and low cost of construction and maintenance. The proviso was made, however, that the incomplete portions of the LBSCR scheme should be finished and brought into operation, although in the event the Streatham–Sutton via Mitcham Junction and the Cheam extensions, on which the least work had been done, were never wired for overhead working.

Work on conversion now began in earnest, and by mid-1925 the first sections of the SECR were electrified, between Victoria and Orpington, round the Catford loop, and to Crystal Palace High Level. A few months earlier, the unfinished parts of the LBSCR overhead scheme between Balham and Coulsdon North, and Selhurst and Sutton, were

Altrincham depot on the Manchester, South Junction and Altrincham Joint line in pre-war days. This line, electrified in 1931 at 1500V dc as a result of the Weir Report to the Ministry of Transport, has now been converted to 25kV ac.

[*W. Hubert Foster*

A train of LNER 1937 North Tyneside articulated stock accelerates away from Manors Station on a stopping service to Whitley Bay from Newcastle Central.

For its 1938 Wirral electrification, the LMS built a number of three-car all-steel units with air-operated sliding doors. One of these handsome units is seen here at Birkenhead North on a Liverpool Central-West Kirby working.

[W. Hubert Foster

completed and brought into use. On the Western Section, the third rail was extended from Claygate to Guildford via Effingham Junction, and from Raynes Park to Dorking North, together with the spur from Leatherhead to Effingham Junction.

Encouraged by the undoubted success of these schemes, the Southern announced in July 1926 its intention to electrify all the remaining suburban lines and, in the cause of standardisation, to convert the Brighton ac overhead lines to the new standard outside third dc system. This goal was achieved in the remarkably short space of four years, the entire suburban systems of the erstwhile South Western, Brighton and South Eastern Railways being electrified on the third rail system, now at 660V, by the end of 1930.

Elsewhere, the prospects for electrification after the Grouping looked much more bleak; the LNER dropped the North Eastern's plan for electrification between Newcastle and York, and no new schemes were proposed elsewhere, apart from an LMS/LNER scheme to electrify the Manchester, South Junction and Altrincham joint line. For this scheme, which was brought into operation in 1931, the 1500V dc overhead system was employed following the recommendation of the Weir Report on Electrification to the Minister of Transport in 1927 that it should be adopted as the new standard.

The early 1930s saw the country in the midst of depression; there was little money about for new investment, and railway electrification schemes were no exception. Apart from the Southern, which managed to maintain the terrific momentum gained during the previous five years, and extended its third rail to Brighton, Eastbourne, Hastings, Worthing and Portsmouth, no new electrification work was carried out until 1938, when the LNER extended its Tyneside third rail system to take in the South Tyneside line through Jarrow to South Shields. In the same year, the LMS introduced electric trains on

As the Southern Railway's third rail electrification spread rapidly in the 1930s, scenes such as this became commonplace. Here, brand-new 2BIL unit No 2147 heads an electric test train through Ascot Station and passes M7 class 0—4—4T No 379 on one of the push-pull workings it was soon to replace.

Showing signs of heavy wartime use, SR 4COR unit No 3136 heads a twelve-car Victoria-Portsmouth buffet express through Clapham Junction in 1949. [*C. C. B. Herbert*

its Wirral suburban lines from Liverpool Central to New Brighton and West Kirby. The outside third 650V dc system of electrification was adopted, but as part of the route was shared with the 650V dc third- and-fourth rail electric trains of the still independent Mersey Railway, the new stock was equipped for both running rail and fourth rail return. This method of working continued until 1956, when the Mersey Railway was converted to third rail operation with running rail return.

After the Second World War, two LNER 1500V dc overhead proposals which had been interrupted by hostilities were completed. The ex-Great Eastern Liverpool Street–Shenfield line was electrified in 1949 (and was extended to Chelmsford and Southend in 1956), while the Manchester-Sheffield line, including a new tunnel at Woodhead, was opened in 1954. In general, however, opinion in the early post-war years swung away from electrification in favour of dieselisation, and no completely new schemes were commenced until the Modernisation Plan appeared in 1955. This proposed that the new standard for electrification should be 25kV ac overhead – an interesting reversion to the thinking behind the early Lancaster-Morecambe-Heysham and Brighton schemes, and a direct contradiction of the Weir Report recommendations of 1927. The plan proposed electrification of the main lines between London, Birmingham, Crewe, Liverpool and Manchester; of the Great Eastern and Tilbury suburban lines from Liverpool Street and Fenchurch Street, including the conversion of the existing 1500V dc equipment; and of the Glasgow Suburban network.

After a lapse of twenty years, the Southern was to be allowed to electrify its Kent Coast lines and, later, the Bournemouth line. Again, in the interests of standardisation, these two schemes were electrified on the SR standard third rail system, the voltage on which had by now been raised to 750V.

These schemes have now all come to fruition, and there is currently a minor revival of interest in railway electrification. The London Midland west coast electrification is being extended northward from Crewe via Carlisle to Glasgow to link with the existing suburban network there, and the original Manchester, South Junction and Altrincham 1500V dc line of 1931 was converted to 25kV ac in 1971 to allow operation of through suburban trains between Crewe and Altrincham. Work is proceeding on the first stage of electrification of the Great Northern suburban services from King's Cross and Moorgate to Letchworth and Hertford North, again at 25kV ac, and work is under way on a new underground in-town loop serving Liverpool Lime Street for the Wirral line trains.

Proposals have been made for the extension of the Wirral system to Hooton and, possibly, Chester, for a southward extension of the Liverpool–Southport line under Liverpool to Central station and on to Hough Green, for a rapid transit system using BR lines in Manchester, and for the re-electrification of the Tyneside lines in the Newcastle area which were so short-sightedly converted to diesel operation less than a decade ago. The Southern Region is hoping to convert all its remaining diesel-worked lines east of Basingstoke and Southampton, plus the Bournemouth–Weymouth line, to electric traction as soon as funds permit.

The fortunes of railway electrification in Britain have been very mixed; once it had been proved to be a reliable form of traction, there was a sudden bout of enthusiasm for suburban electrification immediately before the First World War. Bad post war conditions, then the problems of Grouping, and subsequently the financial problems of the depression, taxed the resources of the 'Big Four'. Only the Southern, serving the most prosperous and least affected part of the country, was willing to press on with further suburban and, later, main line electrification. It is surely ironic that, when main line electrification reached Brighton in January 1933, fifty years after Volks first electric line along the Front, it was by the cheaper third rail system rather than the admittedly more efficient high voltage overhead system originally proposed by the LBSCR. After the Second World War there was a further lull while enthusiasm for dieselisation waxed during the 1950s. But now, electrification has once more come to the fore and is currently enjoying something of a comeback.

Compared with the material produced by the powerful, very vocal and mostly pro-road oil and diesel engine lobbies, the railways have, over the years, received a singular lack of support from the British electrical industry. That the equipment supplied has been of superior design and construction cannot be denied, but for many years there has been little pro-electrification propaganda emanating from the industry, and on more than one occasion this has resulted in a decision against electrification in favour of dieselisation.

Thinking on electrification systems, too, has undergone many changes over the years; in the early days, with much electrical equipment still virtually untried for extended everyday service, and no National Grid to fall back on, most companies opted for low voltage dc. Even in 1927, the Weir Report, while recognising the advantages of higher voltage for long distance transmission, still opted for 1500V dc overhead, and it is only within the last two decades that thinking has reversed in favour of high voltage ac overhead, the main criteria being the thinner section contact wire required, and therefore the lighter weight overhead equipment needed to support it, plus the small number of feeder points required and the lack of substations.

Despite ninety years of progress, however, it seems that the low voltage dc conductor rail system is still the best method of electrification for underground and purely suburban systems, and we can expect it still to be to the fore when railway electrification celebrates its centenary in the next decade.

Great Orme Railway car No 4 descends past Black Gate request stop and heads for the lower terminus at Victoria Station.

[R. W. A. Swain

The Great Orme Railway

R. W. A. SWAIN

The Great Orme Railway is one of Llandudno's 'musts' for holidaymakers, and a ride on it is all the more interesting when one knows how it operates. Many people think of it as a tram like those running along Blackpool promenade, drawing power for traction from the overhead line. Nothing could be further from the truth. The trams on The Great Orme Railway are hauled up the hill by cable, their own weight taking them down again. The railway is in two sections, each having a slightly different method of working, with the winding house at the half-way point.

The lower terminal of the railway is Victoria Station on Church Walks. Car No 4 is housed here at nights, resting against the buffer. There is a ticket office at this station, but tickets are issued on the trams themselves for passengers joining at Half-way and Summit Stations.

From Victoria Station the car ascends Old Road, crosses Ty Gwyn Road and then travels alongside to Half-way Station where the passengers alight and walk past the sheds and winding house to the upper section car waiting to take them on to the summit. This car travels almost straight up The Orme to the Summit Station, crossing the road to St Tudno's Church on the way. Just below the halfway point on each section of the line, the ascending car meets the descending car, there being special passing places at these points.

On each car there is a driver and a conductor. When he is ready to start, the driver at Victoria Station calls the driver of the tram at Half-way Station on his hand-operated telephone to see if he is ready to start. Provided the driver of the other tram is ready, he then presses a bell-push on the cab roof twice – he gives two short rings for a non-stop run to Half-way Station, one long and one short for the request stop at Black Gate, one short and one long to stop at Tyn-y-Coed Road, the other request stop, where the tram turns towards Half Way Station. These signals to the winding house indicate to the engineer that he should stop winding when he has drawn in the length of cable to these points. Of course, when either of these stops is made, the descending car stops as well since the two trams are linked by cable via the winding house. It is for this signalling that the overhead trolley wire is provided, not to supply power to the trams.

When the engineer has been signalled, he releases the brake and sets the winding drums in motion. From Victoria Station the tram ascends the single track line up the very steep and narrow Old Road, the weight of the descending car helping to pull it up the line. The cable which hauls the trams runs in a conduit beneath the road, the tram's drawbar passing through a $1\frac{1}{4}$in slot to reach it. Every six feet there are access covers in the road beside the track. These allow for the inspection of the cable and the lubrication of the vertical steel pulleys which guide it round curves. Horizontally, it runs on grooved sheaves.

From the Old Road, the tram crosses Ty Gwyn Road at Black Gate, the first of the request stops for Llandudno residents. It then proceeds up the hill, running parallel to the road. Shortly, it reaches the passing loop which is just below the half-way point of the lower section of the line. This disparity is due to the fact that the drum for the descending car has paid out more cable per revolution than the drum for the ascending car has taken in, it having previously been fully unwound. At the loop, the line splits into two tracks, and the overhead wire separates as well, to allow the two trams to pass each other. Above the loop, the lines close until the two inner rails share a common centre groove. Below the loop there is only ever one cable in the conduit at a time, but above it there are always two, one drawing in the ascending car, the other paying out behind the one going down. It is because of this that from the passing loop onwards, two separate interlaced tracks are provided. Each has its own conduit, so that the two cables do not foul each other. The conduit widens out at the turnout at the lower end of the loop so as to allow the cable drawbars on the trams to pass through to their respective lines. At night, after the last car down has passed by, a wooden cover is placed over this junction slot. It is, of course, removed before the ascent of the first tram next morning.

Above the junction, each tram always takes the same track, so that the cables do not get crossed. Car No 4 takes the line nearer the road. At Half-way Station, there are three buildings – two tramsheds, with the winding house in the centre housing the cable drums and motors. There are two winding drums each for the lower and upper sections of the line. Each pair is operated by the engineer responsible for that section. The two drums for the lower section can often be seen if the door into the winding house has been left ajar for ventilation on a warm day. The drums in each pair both turn at the same speed, one winding its cable, the other unwinding. As both drums turn in the same direction, the cable is wound round each in opposite ways. This can clearly be seen if, from the tram

Above right: This view of car No 5 descending over the interlaced track towards the lower passing loop illustrates the steeply graded nature of the line.
[R. W. A. Swain

Right: Upper section car No 7 waits outside its shed at Half-way Station whilst passengers from the lower section join for the trip to the summit.
[R. W. A. Swain

5

7 GREAT ORME RAILWAY 7
7

sheds, one looks towards the powerhouse. One cable is horizontal, coming from the base of the drum, as it passes from the winding house to the end of the track in the shed, whilst the other descends quite steeply from the top of its drum.

All the power for the operation of the line and the control equipment comes from the winding house. Prior to 1958, the winding drums were driven by steam, but now the winding gear is powered by two English Electric 415 volt motors. The motor for the lower section drums is of 125hp capacity, whilst that for the upper section drums is only 75hp. This is because the upper section of the line is not so steep and, therefore, requires less power to move the cars.

Apart from the passing loop, the upper section is entirely single track, open all the way except for the level crossing at the road to St Tudno's Church. It is laid on wooden sleepers, there being no conduit. The car drawbars are each mounted off centre to enable the two cables to run within the one track. Each cable runs on its own sheaths and has separate pulleys to guide it. As the winding house is below the summit, the cables work in a different manner from those on the lower section, which just has two, one for each tram. On the upper section there are three cables, one to each tram from the winding house, and a third connecting the two trams via a free-running pulley at the summit. This enables the descending car to pull the ascending car up The Orme. Thus the effect is of one continuous cable running from the winding house via one car to the summit, round the pulley and back via the other car to the winding house.

Until it reaches the passing loop, the track is virtually level, but it rises fairly steeply from here to the plateau at the summit. To overcome any unevenness in the running of the trams and to keep the cable taut, the driver of the descending car keeps his hand brake partly applied until just before entering the loop, the driver of the other car having released his brake by the level crossing.

The passing loop on this section has normal points and as each car leaves the loop it sets the points and overhead wire for its own return. At either end of the loop are the point operating levers, locked in wiremesh cages to prevent tampering. As a further precaution, indicators on the levers indicate for which tram the points are set as each approaches the loop. To allow the cables to pass uninterrupted through the moving lines, there is a suitable gap in each of the inner rails of the turnouts to the loop.

Above the loop the track passes through a short cutting, the steepest part of this section of the line. The ground then levels off as the line reaches Summit Station, 650ft above sea level. At the end of the line is the tramshed where the last tram up at night is housed. To house the upper section cars, the engineer has only to run the cables until the cars are housed, but because the lower section does not have a shed at Victoria Station, part of the downhill cable has to be drawn out at night, by hand, to enable car No 5 to enter its shed.

The four cars operating The Great Orme Railway have all been in use since the line was first opened, the lower section on July 31, 1902, the upper section on July 8, 1903. The lower section trams are painted dark blue, while those on the upper section are blue and cream. All the cars have glazed bulkheads at the ends with sliding doors to enable passengers to enter the saloons. The sides of the cars, however, are unglazed – very pleasant in good weather, but no so popular when it is wet and windy. Bells fitted on the trams warn traffic, people and sheep of approach.

Powerful emergency brakes are fitted to cars 4 and 5 for use in case of mishap on the lower section. These are tested every spring; if a tram starts to run at more than 6¼mph – the operating speed is 5 mph on this section – the emergency brakes come into operation, gripping the concrete alongside the rails, and stopping the car in half its length. The ordinary slipper brakes on the upper section cars are sufficient for emergency use, as this part of the line is not so steep. Water tanks are carried on cars 4 and 5 for watering the track at curves.

All told, the Great Orme Railway is a fascinating (and less tiring!) way to ascend the Great Orme.

The view from an ascending car on the upper section of the Great Orme Railway as it approaches the passing loop and prepares to pass the descending car approaching in the distance.

[D. L. Percival

Llandudno and the bay beyond seen from the front of a descending car on the lower section of the Great Orme Railway. Note the conduit track and, on this section, the common centre rail.

[D. L. Percival

West of Exeter— the Southern's 'Withered Arm'

Ex-LSWR class T9 4—4—0 No 30709 skirts the Camel estuary near Wadebridge on April 6, 1961, with a two-coach train for Padstow, the most westerly station on the Southern Railway's lines west of Exeter, often known as the 'withered arm'. Apart from short sections of line to Wadebridge and Gunnislake, which are still served from the ex-Great Western Plymouth-Truro main line, the 'withered arm' lines west of Okehampton and Barnstaple have all been closed in the past decade.

Exeter Central – Gateway to the Southern's 'Withered Arm'. In this view from the down platform, Z class 0—8—0T No 30953 is assisting N class 2—6—0 No 31844 up the steep bank from Exeter St Davids with a heavy eastbound freight.

[J. B. Bucknall

Class S15 4—6—0 No 30828 prepares to leave the Great Western main line at Cowley Bridge Junction with mixed freight for Plymouth via Okehampton in June, 1959.

[J. F. Loader

Above: With Calstock Viaduct on the Callington branch in the background, Drummond T9 4—4—0 No 30709 climbs away from Bere Alston towards Tavistock with the 10.02am Plymouth-Waterloo train on May 12, 1961. [*S. C. Nash*

Left: On many occasions when the Great Western route was blocked, the Southern route was used for all traffic west of Exeter. On one such occasion in August, 1961, Warship diesel hydraulic No D867 *Zenith* eases the up 'Cornish Riviera Express' down from Meldon Junction onto Meldon viaduct. [*S. C. Nash*

Below: In latter years, there was a considerable amount of inter-working over the GW and SR routes from Exeter to Plymouth. Here, GW 4300 class 2—6—0 No 7316 approaches Meldon Quarry with a down Plymouth freight. [*S. C. Nash*

Right: Unrebuilt Battle of Britain class Pacific No 34054 *Lord Beaverbrook* waits for the road at Bere Alston with the 8.41am Exeter Central-Plymouth Friary train on April 7, 1953. In the background, the Callington branch can be seen curving away to the right.

[R. E. Vincent

Below: With the distant off, rebuilt Battle of Britain class Pacific No 34062 *17 Squadron* skirts Dartmoor near Brentor with the 4.52pm Plymouth-Eastleigh on May 10, 1961.

[S. C. Nash

Above: Barnstaple Junction in August, 1955, with M7 class 0—4—4T No 30255 propelling a train of Great Western stock across the sharply-curved connections to the Ilfracombe line and into the up platform.

[*R. E. Vincent*

Left: West Country class Pacific No 34035 *Shaftesbury* pauses at Lapford with the 4.21pm Exeter Central-Torrington train in the early 1960s.

[*M. E. B. Walters*

Right: Noon on May 29, 1949, finds West Country class Pacific No 34041 *Wilton* storming away from Ilfracombe up the steep bank to Morthoe with the short-lived 'Devon Belle' Pullman car express.

[*C. A. Todhunter*

588
34041
DEVON BELLE
THE
DEVON BELLE

Between trips to Halwill Junction, BR standard class 3 2—6—2T No 82011 shunts wagons at Bude on the last day of June, 1960.

[J. Holmes

In latter years, the Ivatt class 2 2—6—2Ts were regular performers on the Barnstaple-Halwill line. Here No 41210, running bunker first, approaches Fremington with the 12.40pm Torrington-Waterloo train.

[J. C. Beckett

Halwill Junction on August 17, 1963, with N class 2—6—0 No 31838 coming off the single line from Launceston and preparing to cross to the up platform with the 1.05pm Padstow-Okehampton train. The track in the centre foreground is the Bude line and the bay platform to the left served the Torrington branch.
[P. Paye

The line from Torrington to Halwill was built as a light railway in Southern Railway days. It served a very rural part of West Devon and, except in the war years, never boasted much passenger traffic. Here, Ivatt class 2 2—6—2T No 41295 re-starts the afternoon one-coach Torrington-Halwill train from Hatherleigh on September 7, 1960.
[E. T. Gill

Above: In the early days of Nationalisation, N class 2—6—0 No 31833 approaches St Kew Highway with a freight for Wadebridge and Padstow.
[B. A. Butt

Left: Amidst clouds of smoke and steam, O2 class 0—4—4T No 30236 makes a dramatic exit from Wadebridge with the 9.48am train to Bodmin North.
[Brian E. Morrison

Above right: When the Beattie well tanks were finally withdrawn from service on the Wenford Bridge branch in 1962, they were replaced by ex-GWR 1366 class 0—6—0PTs. Here, No 1368 of that class shunts the yard at Wadebridge on August 25, 1962.
[G. D. King

Right: The end of the line: Battle of Britain class Pacific No 34110 *66 Squadron* runs into Padstow with the down 'Atlantic Coast Express'.
[Alan H. Bryant

34110

London Termini: Their Sites and Names

G. T. MOODY

The purely railway history of the London termini is of such importance that it tends to overshadow the origins of their names and the history of their sites, both of which are worthy of more than passing interest.

The senior London terminus is London Bridge, where the initial station was opened by the London & Greenwich Railway as long ago as December 14, 1836. At first there was no train shed but a ramp led down from the end of the viaduct, with the Company's offices on the south side. Additions were soon made to accommodate the trains of the London & Croydon, London & Brighton and South Eastern Railways, and for some years the station was managed by a Joint Committee. In 1850 this was dissolved and the station was divided between the South Eastern and London Brighton & South Coast Railways. In its long history London Bridge underwent a series of drastic alterations. The present 'high level' side was built originally for the South Eastern extension to Charing Cross, opened in 1864. The LBSCR side (now platforms 12–22) was rebuilt and enlarged in 1865–66, and the 'high level' side was treated similarly by the SER in 1893–94 as part of its scheme for widening its London approaches. One of the old train sheds built in the 'forties was used for Continental 'grand vitesse' traffic from 1864 until 1900 when it was demolished and replaced by the South Eastern & Chatham 'low level' station (now platforms 8–11), opened on June 2, 1902. The large and ornate Terminus Hotel was built on the south side of the LBSCR station and opened in 1861, but it proved unsuccessful, and in 1893 it was taken over for use as offices, a function which continued under the Southern Railway until it was destroyed by bombing in 1940. The whole of the large area of the combined stations is built on brick arches, most of which are let as cellarage. A public thoroughfare – Joiner Street – runs through them from St Thomas's Street to Tooley Street. Remains of the earlier stations are now confined to structures below station level, but the frontage buildings on the 'high level' side were built before 1850. The origin of the station's name is obvious, as it is close to the southern end of London Bridge, but it may well be asked why *London* Bridge. The answer is that until about 1750 there was only one bridge across the Thames in London, hence its name. The recently demolished stone bridge was opened by William IV in state on August 1, 1831, and was therefore still quite new when the first station was opened.

Cannon Street station was opened by the SER on September 1, 1866. John Stow, the Elizabethan antiquary and writer, whose 'Survey' gave us much of our knowledge of ancient London, tells us that in his time the thoroughfare on which the station abuts was called Candlewright Street, as it was once inhabited by candle makers, an important craft in those times. Its present title is an example of the corruption of place names often found in London.

The area covered by the station includes the site of the Steelyard, the London house of the German Hanse merchants for three centuries, and of St Mary Bothaw, one of the City churches not rebuilt after the Great Fire of 1666. Both are commemorated by plaques on the station frontage. Cannon Street is the nearest main line terminus to the 'Bank', centre of the City of London.

The station is 685ft long by 202ft wide, and the now demolished semi-circular roof, for many years a prominent feature of the City skyline, was 120ft high. Its construction was a massive piece of work, involving the use of 31 million bricks and 2,000 tons of ironwork for the roof. Another 12,000 tons of ironwork were needed for the five spans of the approach

Cannon Street in May 1958, and already work has begun on dismantling the overall roof as Schools Class 4—4—0 No 30913 *Christ's Hospital* sets out with the 5.06pm commuter train to Hastings.
[*R. C. Riley*

bridge across the Thames. The ornate frontage building was originally a large hotel, the great hall of which was a popular place for company meetings, including those of the Southern Railway. It was converted to offices in 1932.

Also in the City, the London Chatham & Dover Railway to Ludgate Hill was opened on December 21, 1864. Lud Gate was one of the ancient City gates, so called from an early, possibly mythical, King Lud. The continuation to the Metropolitan Railway at Farringdon Street, opened on January 1, 1866, occupied part of the site of the notorious Fleet Prison for debtors, which figures prominently in Charles Dickens' *Pickwick Papers*. The terminus at Holborn Viaduct was not opened until March 2, 1874; like Cannon Street, its frontage was originally a large hotel, opened on November 17, 1877. It, too, was converted to offices after World War I, and was destroyed by enemy action in 1941. The 'Viaduct' from which the station takes its name was one of the great metropolitan improvements carried out between 1860–70, to obviate the steep descents into the valley of the old Fleet River. It was opened to traffic on November 8, 1869, and the first vehicle to cross it was a 'City-Atlas' bus en route to London Bridge station. The third LCDR City station – St Pauls – was opened on May 10, 1886. On February 1, 1937, it was renamed 'Blackfriars', a much more suitable title, as it corresponded with that of the 'Underground' station below, and the adjacent bridge. The name originated from the monastery of the Black (or Dominican) Friars which stood in the vicinity from the 13th to the 16th century. It may be added that Ludgate Hill station was rebuilt in 1907–10, and was closed by the Southern Railway on March 3, 1929, although the dilapidated remains of its island platform still survive.

Queen Eleanor, wife of Edward I, died near Lincoln in 1297, and her body was brought to Westminster Abbey for burial. At each place where the cortege halted the King had a memorial erected, known as an 'Eleanor Cross'. The last of these was situated in the village of Charing, between London and

Westminster, and thus became known as Charing Cross. It was destroyed by the Roundheads in 1647.

Sir Edward Hungerford, a spendthrift courtier of Charles II, obtained a royal licence to build a market on part of his estate near Charing Cross, which was opened in 1682. 'Hungerford Market' was never very successful. It was rebuilt in 1831–33, and with a view to attracting custom from the Surrey side of the river, powers were obtained in 1836 to build a toll footbridge. This bridge was not completed until 1845; it was of suspension type, designed by I. K. Brunel, and consisted of two side spans and a centre span of 676ft, resting on red brick piers in the river bed.

The Act authorising the SER extension from London Bridge to Charing Cross also provided for the purchase of the market and the bridge. The former was demolished and the new terminus built on its site. The chains from the latter were used in the construction of the famous suspension bridge over the Avon gorge near Bristol, while the brick piers were incorporated in the present railway bridge. The footpath on the down side of the latter is still known as 'Hungerford Bridge'; a toll was charged for its use until 1878. Charing Cross station was a smaller edition of Cannon Street with a similar semi-circular iron roof, 170ft in span and 98ft high. It partly collapsed during repairs on December 5, 1905 and the station was closed for four months while the rest of the old roof was removed; it was subsequently replaced by the present flat roof. Charing Cross was opened for local trains on January 11, 1864, and for all trains on the following May 1, but the large hotel which forms the frontage was not opened until May 15, 1865. Its architect, E. M. Barry, designed a replica of the Eleanor Cross which was erected in the forecourt and is still to be seen there.

In 1809 the Strand Bridge Co was empowered to build a toll bridge across the Thames, and the Act also provided for laying out the present Waterloo Road to connect the new bridge with existing thoroughfares at St Georges Circus, Southwark. By a later Act the name was changed to Waterloo Bridge, to commemorate the battle of Waterloo, fought and won on June 18, 1815, while the bridge was being built. Exactly two years later the bridge was opened by the Prince Regent (later King George IV) accompanied by the Duke of Wellington. It was not freed from toll until 1878.

The original terminus of the London & South Western Railway, at Nine Elms and close to the river side, was opened on May 21, 1838. The City, over 3 miles away, was reached by buses and the many small steamers which then plied on the Thames. This position soon proved unsatisfactory, and in 1845 powers were obtained to extend the line from a point near the present Queens Road station to a point near Hungerford Bridge. The Act was unopposed owing to the poor class of the locality through which the extension passed – the site of the terminus is said to have been occupied by 'haystalls, cow yards, dung heaps and other nuisances.' Four lines were provided on the extension, built on brick arches and laid out on a series of sweeping curves to avoid Vauxhall Gardens (a famous pleasure resort, closed in 1859), the grounds of Lambeth Palace, and a gasworks. The cost is said to have been £900,000. It was completed by June, 1848, but opening was delayed until the Board of Trade Inspecting Officer was satisfied with the stability of the bridge over Westminster Bridge Road, and the first train did not enter the three platform terminus until the early morning of July 13, 1848. Permanent station buildings were not erected until 1853, for at first the terminus was regarded as an intermediate station on a further extension to London Bridge. Powers for this were obtained in 1846, but the project was abandoned owing to the financial crisis of 1848. In its early days the station was often known as 'Waterloo Bridge' and the present title – Waterloo – was not generally used

Night-time at Waterloo, and a somewhat grimy West Country class Pacific, No 34023 *Blackmore Vale*, lets off steam impatiently as it waits for the road to the west.

[Dr. L. A. Nixon

WB.174
WB.173

until 1886. The station was enlarged in 1862, 1879 and 1885, the last mentioned addition surviving as the present platforms 16–21. The older parts disappeared during the complete rebuilding from 1902–22. Its proximity to the terminus is no doubt the reason why the parish church of St John, Waterloo Road, was said to be the scene of more runaway marriages than any other church in London!

Thomas Cubitt, the great London builder, leased the marshy area known as the 'Five Fields' from Lord Grosvenor, and from about 1825 it was drained, made up (largely with soil excavated from St Katharine's Docks) and built over to become the present day area of Belgravia. At the same time the Grosvenor Canal was cut from the Thames near Chelsea Hospital to a large basin about a mile north. This period was also one of great development in the layout of Westminster; slums were cleared, Victoria Street laid out in 1845–51, and new buildings of good class erected.

In anticipation of heavy traffic from the West End to the Crystal Palace (opened in 1854), as well as to relieve congestion at London Bridge, then the only London terminus of the LBSCR, the West End of London & Crystal Palace Railway (worked by, and later merged with, the Brighton) was incorporated in 1853 to build lines from Norwood Junction to Crystal Palace and then to a terminus on the south side of the river at Battersea. These were opened in 1856–58. In the latter year the Victoria Station & Pimlico Railway was authorised to continue this line across the river and to enter into an agreement with the LBSCR to build approach lines and clear a site for the latter to erect a terminus. The upper end of the Grosvenor Canal and the basin were taken over, drained and used as the site for the approach lines and the new terminus. In consequence the foundations of the new station and the adjoining Grosvenor Hotel had to be laid on piles. The new station, 1000ft long by 480ft wide and named Victoria in honour of the Queen, was opened on October 1, 1860. It was used by LCDR trains from December 3, 1860, until the adjoining terminus, leased by the Victoria Station & Pimlico to the LCD and Great Western Railways, was opened on August 25, 1862. The lease lasted until the formation of the Southern Railway in 1923, and a regular service of GW trains ran from 1863 to 1915. To meet local objections to steam and smoke from engines, the approach lines were originally covered by a glass and iron roof.

The Grosvenor Hotel, at the north-western corner of the LBSCR station, was opened in 1861; its site was 262ft long by 75ft wide and it contained 300 rooms. The LBSCR took over the station and approach lines from the VSPR in 1862. Originally only wooden buildings were erected on the frontage of both stations. The LBSCR side was completely rebuilt and enlarged between 1902 and 1908; 1200 piles had to be driven for the foundations of the new frontage building, the upper floors of which were an annex of 150 rooms to the Grosvenor Hotel. At the same time the LCDR station was also provided with new frontage buildings. A public house close to the terminus is still called 'The Grosvenor Basin', and a short piece of the canal remains and is used by the City of Westminster for barging refuse.

The Great Western Railway was originally authorised to join the London & Birmingham Railway near Wormwood Scrubs, the two lines to share a common London terminus, but as negotiations between the two companies broke down, the Great Western secured powers in 1836 to extend its line to a point near the village of Paddington, then on the verge of London and still quite rural in character. Land in the vicinity belonged to the Bishopric of London, and when the first section of the line was opened on June 4,

Above right: The 'Eastern' part of Victoria, with Rebuilt Merchant Navy class Pacific No 35023 *Holland Afrika Line* coming to a stand at Platform 2 with an enthusiasts' special from Templecombe on March 28, 1965.

[*Brian Stephenson*

Right: Beneath Brunel's impressive arched roof, Castle class 4—6—0 No 7006 *Lydford Castle* simmers gently at the buffers on Platform 9 after arrival with a train from Worcester.

[*Eric Treacy*

35023

9
7006

1838, trains started from a temporary station on the west side of Bishops (now Bishops Bridge) Road. Other property in the neighbourhood – Westbourne Park – belonged to Lord Hill, hence the name of 'Lord Hill's Bridge'. It was not until 1850 that it was decided to build a permanent station. Designed by I. K. Brunel, it consisted of three semi-circular spans, 700ft long by 238ft wide, and was opened in 1854, the departure side on January 16, and the arrival side on May 29. The hotel on the frontage was opened on June 9. The platforms used by Metropolitan trains were known as Bishops Road from 1863 until they were rebuilt and incorporated into the main terminus in 1933.

Marylebone, the last London terminus to be built and one of the smallest, with only four platforms, was opened by the Great Central Railway on March 15, 1899. A large amount of poor class property was pulled down to provide the site; the name was taken from that of the locality and borough. This was itself a corruption of St Mary-le-bourne, the name given to the old parish church which stood on the bank of one of the streams which flowed to the Thames in former times. The red brick station buildings were separated from the main road by the large Hotel Great Central, which shared the fate of other terminal hotels in being converted subsequently to offices, and is now occupied by the Headquarters of the British Railways Board.

Originally the London & Birmingham Railway was authorised to terminate at Camden Town, but in 1835 powers were obtained to extend the line to a terminus in the parish of St. Pancras, close to what was then known as the 'New Road'. Land in this neighbourhood belonged to the Duke of Grafton and was used as nursery gardens until it was built over in the first quarter of the 19th century. As the Duke was also Earl of Euston, and his seat is at Euston Hall, Thetford, Norfolk, it was natural that three of the new thoroughfares should be named Euston Grove, Euston Square and Euston Street. The terminus of the London & Birmingham Railway facing Euston Square was opened on July 29, 1837, and comprised only arrival and departure platforms with intervening sidings. The Company purchased sufficient ground to provide a terminus for Great Western trains, but as already men-

Royal Scot 4—6—0 No 46128 *The Lovat Scouts* brings the up 'Lakes Express' to a stand at Platform 1 at Pre-Electrification Euston on September 1, 1962
[Brian Stephenson

tioned this part of the scheme did not materialise. The monumental 'Doric Arch' which formed the entrance to the station was not finished until 1838, and its wrought iron gates exhibited the coat of arms of the original company until it was demolished to make way for the new station in the last decade. It was not long before additional platforms and offices were provided, and further additions made after the formation of the London & North Western Railway in 1846 included the imposing 'Great Hall,' 128ft long, with its large ornamental ceiling copied from a church in Rome. It was opened in 1849 and remained in use until it, too, disappeared during the 'modernisation' of the 1960s. Considerable extensions were made between 1871 and 1873 and again between 1887 and 1892.

Railways are sometimes accused of making slums but before King's Cross and St Pancras stations were built the area was very indifferent in character. At one time it was known as Battle Bridge, and there is still a Battle Bridge Road. Tradition has it that it was the scene of the defeat of Queen Boadicea and her army by the Romans about 60 AD. A building put up at the nearby crossroads was inscribed 'King's Cross. Erected by subscription in honor of George IV. 1830'. It was topped by an indifferent statue of that monarch and in its life of only 15 years was used for several purposes, including a police station and a beerhouse. The locality thus became known as King's Cross, and the title was adopted by the Great Northern Railway for its terminus, built on the site of a smallpox hospital and rubbish tip, and opened on October 14, 1852. The cost was £123,000 and the stark severity of the buildings reflects the difficulties which beset railways after the financial crash of 1848. Originally there were only arrival and departure platforms, separated by a number of carriage sidings.

The site of St Pancras was a slum of the worst kind, known as 'Agar Town,' from the name of its former landowner. As part of the site for its new line, the Midland Railway took over a piece of the large burial ground

The impressive frontage buildings of St Pancras Station seen from the steps of the connecting stairway to nearby King's Cross. Originally built as a hotel and then used as offices, the structure is now mostly empty. [*John Vaughan*

1A16

surrounding the old parish church dedicated to St Pancras, the boy martyr of the Diocletian persecution of 304 AD, and took that name for its new terminus opened on October 1, 1868. It was appropriate, therefore, that the new station buildings should be designed by Sir Gilbert Scott, a famous church architect. Their elaborate decoration is in complete contrast to King's Cross, and a prominent feature is the arched roof of 240ft span. The cellarage below the station was specially designed for the storage of ale from Burton-on-Trent. The hotel which formed the frontage was not completed until May 5, 1873, and as far as possible the materials used were produced on the Midland system. It, too, failed to pay its way as a hotel in due course, and became offices in 1935.

The Bethlehem Hospital for the Insane (better known in later years as 'Bedlam') stood on the site of Liverpool Street station from the 13th century until 1676, when it was transferred to new buildings in Moorfields. In 1815 it was moved again, to new premises in Lambeth. When the locality was redeveloped, the new street was named after the Prime Minister of the day, Lord Liverpool. Apart from its transport associations, Liverpool Street has never been a prominent City thoroughfare, and this was probably the reason why the terminus of the North London Railway, opened on November 1, 1865, was named after the better known Broad Street, although it actually faced Liverpool Street. The Great Eastern terminus was named Liverpool Street from its opening for local trains on February 2, 1874, although the Metropolitan station opposite was known as Bishopsgate from its opening on July 12, 1875, until it was renamed Liverpool Street on January 1, 1909. 'Bishopsgate' was strictly incorrect, as that thoroughfare was known for many years after the station opened as Bishopsgate Street Within or Without, according to its relation to the site of the old City gate, traditionally built by an early Bishop of London. Main line trains used the new Liverpool Street terminus from November 1, 1875. A congested area of narrow streets and alleys was cleared away to form the site of the station and its approaches, and as the alternative to rehousing the displaced population the Great Eastern Railway agreed to provide workmen's trains at very cheap fares from Edmonton and Walthamstow. The original station comprised the present platforms 1–10 and cost about £2 million. Critics regarded it as a large white elephant and doubted whether there would ever be enough traffic to justify it. The traffic grew so fast, however, that within ten years it was apparent that further accommodation would be needed. Eventually the 'East Side' (platforms 11–18) was built and opened on April 2, 1894. Among the property pulled down to make room for this extension was a Jacobean house built for Sir Paul Pindar, a wealthy City merchant who was Ambassador to Turkey from 1611–20. Its frontage was transferred to the Victoria & Albert Museum.

This tour concludes at Fenchurch Street, appropriately reached from that thoroughfare by the short Railway Place. The station was originally built by the London & Blackwall Railway and opened on August 2, 1841. It was altered in 1853 and rebuilt by the GER in 1882; its five platforms were reduced to four when the interior was rearranged in 1934–35. Stow tells us that Fenchurch Street took its name from a church – St Gabriel – which stood in fenny, or swampy ground. The Blackwall Railway was originally intended to provide facilities for City merchants and shipowners to reach what were then the principal London docks, the East and West India, and it may be noted that shipping interests are still prominent in Fenchurch Street and its vicinity.

Above left: The overall roof of St Pancras 'Train Shed' is now the subject of a preservation order. Here, an LMS class 4F 0–6–0 struggles away with a heavy special boat train for Tilbury in June, 1951. Note the LNWR-type signals on the extreme right. [*British Railways*

Left: Always a cramped and somewhat austere terminus, King's Cross is now being resignalled and modernised in connection with suburban electrification. In this view, surprisingly taken almost a decade ago, 'Deltic' No D9000 *Royal Scots Grey* pulls away from Platform 8 with the down 'Flying Scotsman'. [*Eric Treacy*

West Country Pacific No 34001 banks a Weymouth–Waterloo train past Upwey Wishing Well in June 1967. The last coach is a post World War II SR brake third, one of the first Bulleid designs with side doors to each compartment. Next to it is a later Bulleid type with end doors. [*Derek Cross*

Fifty Years of Railway Carriage Design

G. M. KICHENSIDE

The many companies which made up the British railway scene at the opening of the 1920s had had little chance to recover from the effects of World War I by the time the reorganisation which was to be caused by the Grouping was being planned and passed through Parliament. As a result, on many railways, mechanical design, particularly of passenger rolling stock, continued unchanged from the types in production before and during the war. Indeed, had they but known it, some companies had established designs during the Edwardian period which were to last them until the end of their separate existence. London & North Western and Great Northern designs, for example, showed little difference other than in detail between coaches built in 1910 and those built in 1920. In contrast, the Midland, which had employed the clerestory roof almost continuously for its long distance stock from the late 1890s until the end of the First World War, abandoned it in favour of the elliptical roof in new stock built from about 1917.

The Great Western, which had employed distinctive toplights above compartment windows in its coaches built from about 1905, abandoned them from about 1920 and, moreover, abolished the bodyside mouldings which served the dual purpose of covering joins between panels and forming a base for decorative lining, in some steel-panelled stock built from 1923 onwards.

It was in the South of England that the greatest design change occurred when the South Eastern & Chatham, a line which had

For more than 30 years GWR main line corridor coach types changed little in basic side corridor layout but constructional methods developed from all-timber bodies to the timber-framed steel-panelled style of the wide body composite (*top*) built in 1929. Not until the mid-1930s did the GW introduce corridor coaches with end doors, typified by the brake third of 1935 (*above*).
[*British Railways*

clung to non-gangwayed coaches for all its services, with the exception of a few corridor brake tri-composites for through services to other parts of the country, suddenly blossomed forth with some new corridor coaches for its Folkestone and Dover boat trains, quite unlike anything that had ever run before on the SECR. They had straight match-boarded sides and high elliptical roofs by comparison with the low roofs of standard SECR stock; while most of these new coaches had through gangways the brake coaches were fitted with gangways at one end only, which made it inconvenient in later years if additional corridor vehicles were marshalled outside the brake van. Fortunately the Southern Railway as successor to the SECR was far more disciplined in the operation of set formation trains than its counterparts in the rest of the country.

Thus at the grouping in 1923 the four new companies inherited a motley collection of carriages from the smaller concerns which they had taken over. They ranged from the sumptuous 12-wheel sleeping and dining cars of the West Coast route to the newly-built four-wheelers which the Caledonian was still turning out for some of its Glasgow area suburban services, even though bogie vehicles had been standardised by many companies from the turn of the century.

Electricity had been used for carriage lighting from its early beginnings in the 1880s and 1890s, yet the Great Western and the Midland were still building gas-lit stock until a few years before the grouping, so that only a small proportion of both companies' coaches were electrically lit. The Midland and the LMS paid the penalty in a number of train fires following accidents in which escaping gas was ignited.

Only the Great Western had any continuity

of design before and after the grouping, since the company continued virtually unchanged in the 1923 reorganisation and merely absorbed smaller railways. On the LNER, Gresley of the Great Northern Railway took over the mechanical engineering reins with the result that Great Northern designs – with detail improvements – gradually dominated those of the other constituents. Reid of the Midland succeeded to the position of carriage superintendent of the LMS and it was not surprising that LMS coach design followed Midland patterns. On the Southern completely fresh carriage designs appeared, for the first SR standard coaches showed little affinity to anything that had gone before except possibly to the last type of London & South Western corridor coach, but even then there were marked differences. The Southern was also unique in that throughout its existence it did not produce any new non-corridor locomotive-hauled coaches. In its first years it did not need to, since all three of its principal constituents had relied extensively on non-gangwayed coaches for the majority of services. Indeed, with the few exceptions already noted and one or two other oddities the South Eastern & Chatham and Brighton companies did not possess any gangwayed vehicles and, apart from the Bournemouth and Exeter line expresses, most trains on the LSW were formed of non-gangwayed stock. True, all three companies made extensive use of coaches equipped with between-compartment toilets, but generally speaking, the main line corridor train was a rarity in Southern England.

Because of the relatively short distances

To mark the company's centenary the GWR built new sets of coaches for the 'Cornish Riviera Express' in 1935 (*below*). They had recessed end doors and 9ft 7in wide bodies with large drop windows in each compartment. Following World War II, the GWR adopted a new design which included a domed roof, end and side doors, and windows with sliding top window ventilators as on this corridor third (*foot*). The corridor window spacing, however, was irregular and presented an untidy appearance.

[*British Railways*

Until World War II the Southern standardised side corridor designs with doors to each compartment and matching doors and windows on the corridor side; this Maunsell brake third (*top*) also shows the recessed sides of the guards and luggage compartment. In contrast is a Bulleid corridor composite of 1945 (*above*) showing the end and centre door layout and the deep windows with sliding window ventilators in compartments. Notice the continuously curved steel bodyside.

[British Railways

between London and the South Coast, the area served by the newly-formed Southern Railway was admirably suited to electrification which was undertaken over a period during the following 40 or so years. As each new route was electrified so new corridor trains, many including refreshment facilities, were built. Even for its London area suburban electric conversions, the Southern only needed to build two relatively small batches of new non-corridor stock in its early years, because most of the early suburban electric trains were obtained by rebuilding old four- and six-wheel, and bogie coach bodies on new underframes. In later years the position was reversed when the wooden bodies became life-expired and the Southern put new steel bodies on the by-now secondhand underframes after World War II.

The LNER built large quantities of non-corridor stock, particularly for its London area suburban services, and many of the coaches were articulated in pairs or in groups of four or five. Indeed, Gresley was an advocate of articulation, which not only saved weight but economised on the number of bogies per train. The main disadvantage was that if a defect developed on one coach the whole unit had to be taken out of service. While articulation did not lend itself to the longer distance trains because formations needed to be more flexible to cope with traffic variations, Gresley built some three-coach articulated restaurant-car units. Gresley was also an advocate of electric cooking in kitchen cars, the first of which appeared in 1922. The LMS in contrast could never get on with electric cooking and continued to use gas for cooking and lighting in its kitchen cars until the mid-1930s.

During the early 1930s LMS coach design underwent considerable changes, for in a period of no more than four years the side-door coach gave way to end doors, and then timber bodies were replaced by steel-panelled bodies, although retaining wooden framing. These design changes occurred as a result of a change at the top when the LMS mechanical engineering department went through some years of uncertainty, culminating in the appointment of William Stanier as chief mechanical engineer, who brought from the Great Western sound practice, and established years of stability in the LMS motive power and carriage departments. Indeed, many consider that Stanier initiated some of the finest products ever to appear on a British railway; the carriage designs were simple and neat, and introduced deep windows with sliding window ventilators in the upper part, a feature which continued with little change until the present time.

The LMS made extensive use of open coaches, that is with centre corridor and seats dispersed on each side. Indeed, this practice started in the 1920s with the construction of large quantities of wooden-bodied coaches with end vestibule doors, and distinguished by twin windows to each seating bay. Such were the demands of the LMS carriage building programme that the LMS workshops could not keep pace, despite a reorganisation of Derby Works to turn out wooden body coaches on mass-production lines in the mid-1920s, and more than 200 coaches with all-steel bodies were built by outside contractors. Yet although the advantages of all-steel body construction were recognised from these and other isolated examples, timber body construction, later with steel outside body panelling, remained standard on all four British railways until the end of their separate existence in 1947. It was simply a question of economics – timber was cheaper than steel at that time.

During the 1920s and 1930s three of the four companies, the LNER, LMS and Great Western, produced some special vehicles for running in their principal named expresses. The LNER from time to time built new sets for its Flying Scotsman train including such gimmicks as hairdressing saloons, cinema and ladies retiring room. In 1928, the LMS produced a lounge car for the Royal Scot service and in 1935 the LNER built the first of its mid 1930s streamlined special trains for the Silver Jubilee service. In the same year the Great Western built new trains of wide-body coaches for the Cornish Riviera Express to mark the centenary of the Great Western Railway Company. The 9ft 7in wide bodies were allowed by the generous clearances bequeathed by the broad gauge even after its abandonment in 1892.

In 1937 the LMS and LNER introduced their Coronation Scot and Coronation trains respectively, which in the case of the former were standard vehicles rebuilt with more luxurious interiors. The LNER streamlined trains featured new interior decor, including rexine and painted interiors instead of wood graining. The Coronation train also included an observation car at the back. All these services were short-lived, however, for the second world war stopped all the high-speed services.

All four group companies took advantage of the Second World War to think out improvements in coaching stock design. In the case of the LMS and Great Western changes were more in detail, including the introduction of steel framing in the case of the former. Indeed, the LMS had conducted some interesting experiments in the years immediately preceding the war in new constructional methods, including new Coronation Scot coaches built in 1939 and 1946, and had built batches of integral-construction lightweight electric coaches for the Liverpool–Southport and Wirral lines. On the LNER the new Chief Mechanical Engineer, Thompson, swept away Gresley's designs and introduced new

For most of the Southern Railway suburban electrification schemes of the 1920s and 1930s, old pre-grouping coach bodies, 8ft wide, were rebuilt on new underframes; illustrated is a former LBSCR coach nearer the camera, marshalled next to a Bulleid 9ft wide all-steel coach of the post World War II period. The difference in width can be seen clearly.

[*G. M. Kichenside*

The only non-gangwayed suburban coaches built new by the Southern Railway were two batches of stock constructed in 1925 for electrification to Guildford and Orpington. Illustrated is part of one of the Eastern Section units.

[*G. M. Kichenside*

Above: The LMS built large numbers of wooden-bodied open coaches during the 1920s; they were similar to earlier Midland designs with twin windows to each seating bay, and end doors and toilets. Open third No 1324 (*below*) was of a later LMS design, employed only for a year or so about 1930, but which was important, for it represented a transition phase having a timber body but with wide, deep windows.

[*British Railways*

Below: During the mid-1920s, the LMS ordered over 200 open coaches from private industry; they had all-steel bodies but were generally similar to the wooden bodied twin-window designs, even to the painted lining representing panels.

[*British Railways*

steel-sided coaches, some of which showed marked differences in layout than earlier types. Corridor coaches, for example, had external doors and cross vestibules placed towards the middle of the coach so that the compartments were divided into groups of two or three, thus avoiding the need for passengers in the middle of the coach to pass more than one other compartment to reach an outside door.

The greatest change, however, was seen on the Southern Railway where Bulleid, who had succeeded Maunsell in 1938, produced some revolutionary (for the Southern) suburban electric and main line steam-hauled coaches. Body sides were continuously curved from the rain strip above the windows to the underside of the body, and body panels and framing were of welded construction. Suburban electric passengers found that seats extended to the inner face of the outside body panelling sheets, thus accommodating six passengers side by side in each compartment, a feature almost unknown on the Southern until then, although adopted by the Great Eastern as long ago as 1900.

Bulleid's ingenious frame of mind did not stop at trying to cram even more commuters side by side in sardine cans, for he also attempted experiments with coaches that would pack them in two layers as well with his double-deck suburban trains built in 1949. Their principal disadvantage was the time taken in loading and unloading and no more than two four-car units were built. Bulleid was not the only British carriage designer to think in terms of a double-deck train, for Stanier evolved such a design in the late 1930s, although it never saw the light of day.

Except on the Southern, where Bulleid's designs were built in large quantities, the post second world war types of the other three railways were not built extensively, although they continued to be constructed for a few years after 1948 when the four group companies were Nationalised to form British Railways.

The first British Railways standard coaches appeared in 1951. Outwardly they did not resemble any of the types produced by the four group companies, although they showed certain affinities to the Bulleid post-war coaches on the Southern, for they had continuously curved sides, but the steel panels were flattened around the windows to allow the fitting of flat glass in contrast to the Bulleid coaches in which the window glass followed the contour of the sides. A standard length underframe of 63ft 5in over headstocks was used for all corridor passenger coaches

After World War II, the LMS again ventured into all-steel body designs in its corridor composites with porthole toilet windows. These coaches were delivered after Nationalisation and did not appear with the LMS insignia.

[*British Railways*

Although Gresley designed a number of coach types with end doors, particularly during the 1930s for special services, the ordinary standard LNER main line type until World War II was the side-door corridor compartment coach; illustrated (*top*) is a brake composite. In contrast (*above*) is a Thompson post-war corridor composite in which the doors were positioned towards the coach centre. Compartments had deep windows with sliding ventilator windows, and toilets were distinguished by large oval windows.

[*G. M. Kichenside*

and a shorter length of 56ft 11in for most non-gangwayed vehicles, although some of the latter were built on the longer underframe. The non-gangwayed coaches were thus virtually identical in length with their LMS 57ft counterparts. Corridor coaches were generally longer than the pre-Nationalisation stock, except the post-war Bulleid coaches, which were virtually identical in length. Most LNER corridor coaches were on 60ft underframes, while the majority of LMS ordinary corridor vehicles were 57ft long, although some were 60ft or 62ft in length. In contrast, the massive LMS 12-wheel restaurant and sleeping cars carried on six-wheel bogies were 68ft and 69ft long respectively, almost as long as the Great Western's 70-footers. Over the years the Great Western had built some quite lengthy coaches and as far back as 1905 had produced vehicles 70ft or so long and 9ft 7in wide for use on its principal ex-broad gauge main lines. At various times the GW had built batches of long and wide coaches, but intermittently there were batches of shorter length, generally 60ft in pre-war days and 63ft in the post second world war period and widths varied between 8ft 11in and 9ft 7 in.

BR non-gangwayed designs included some

relatively new patterns, including open third class coaches with and without toilet facilities but retaining side doors to each seating bay. A feature of all new standard BR coaches was the all-welded steel body construction which, welded to the underframe, provided a strong box structure. Another standard feature adopted for corridor stock was the buckeye coupler, hitherto used only by the LNER and Southern to any extent.

In general layout and decor the new standard coaches did not show much advance on previous practice but during the 1950s new materials, including plastic laminate panels, replaced grained veneers. Double glazing was introduced on a limited scale, and because of unsatisfactory riding given by the original standard bogie new bogie types appeared, all measures which helped to increase the weight to as much as 37 tons by comparison with the 30–34 tons of earlier coaches. Some of the double-glazing experiments could hardly be called successful. Air leaks and condensation between panes, particularly on BR electric stock built for the Southern, caused water to build up, often to a depth of several inches, at the bottom of the windows.

The mid 1950s saw the widespread introduction of a new type of train, the diesel multiple-unit. These were self-contained units of two, three, four or more coaches, with driving cabs at each end with a proportion of vehicles in each set equipped with (usually) underfloor diesel engines. Most types of diesel multiple unit were of somewhat lighter construction than locomotive-hauled coaches and sported rather utilitarian internal layouts with bus-type seating; they were employed on local and branch services. A few designs, however, were for main line work and in these the coaches were generally similar to long distance locomotive-hauled stock.

Diesel trains,while new to British Railways, were not the first of their type in Great Britain, for the Great Western had used diesel railcars, generally running singly, on a number of branch and local services during the 1930s.

In 1957 British Railways called on a number of carriage building firms to produce new ideas for locomotive-hauled stock in some prototype vehicles built to try out new layouts, seats, decor and ventilation. With one exception, few of the ideas advanced were adopted for general production. The exception, in certain design characteristics, including the wide sealed double-glazed windows, semi-reclining seats and modern decor, was the design by Cravens of two coaches which in retrospect showed remarkable similarities with the diesel and electric Pullmans built in the following decade.

While BR coach design did not show any immediate change during the early 1960s, new designs appeared embodying integral construction, lighter weight, new seats and modern decor in what became known as the Mark II fleet. Some of the new ideas were first displayed in a special prototype train known as Project XP64 built in 1964, including wider folding entrance doors, new bogies and many other facets. Again, some of the prototype features were not adopted for the main batches but the Mark II fleet introduced several new principles, one of which directly affected passengers, for no more side corridor second class (third class was renamed second in 1956) were to be built and all second class accommodation in future was to be in open saloons. Later batches of the Mark II fleet stock embodied wide entrance doors, 3ft compared with the original 2ft width, but unlike the XP64 type, of a one-piece design which wrapped round the coach end.

Succeeding batches included a number of improved amenities, among them better sound and heat insulation and pressure ventilation, culminating in 1971 with full air conditioning, which swept away the need for opening windows in the passenger saloons and compartments. British Railways was the first in the world to embark on air conditioning for ordinary non-supplement trains. Air conditioning itself was not new and was adopted for luxury trains overseas more than 20 years before. Indeed, BR had used full air conditioning in the luxury diesel multiple-unit Pullman trains running on the London Midland and Western Regions from 1960 and the locomotive-hauled Pullmans built for the LMR electrification in 1966. These coaches introduced new standards of luxury far exceeding anything that had been built before in Britain and were the equal of the best trains in Europe.

British Railways have given the world a lead and during the next few years we shall see a new generation of coaches, the Mark III, for the 125 mph high speed diesel train units, and the tilting body coaches for the 150 mph advanced passenger train project. If the Channel Tunnel is built, the new generation coaches will include types for cross-Channel services to other parts of Europe. We have come a long way from the gaslit wooden-bodied compartment coaches of the 1920s to the spacious air conditioned saloons of the present day. One can only hope that future BR carriage design does not progress backwards, for already certain features are becoming apparent – smaller windows awkwardly placed for comfort, and plans for new seating layouts which may not coincide with windows – perhaps insignificant details to today's trendy designers but important features to passengers who like to see the countryside, even if it is passing at 150 mph.

The first all-steel BR designs followed to some extent the last Southern patterns, with a continuously curved bodyside, but with detail differences; illustrated (*below*) is an open third of the early 1950s. Twenty years later, in 1971, BR introduced air-conditioned coaches to ordinary services (*foot*). No longer was there a need for opening windows and ventilators but for constructional reasons windows were much shallower than hitherto. Another feature, also found on earlier batches of these Mark II coaches, was the wrap-round end door, giving a 3ft wide opening.

[*British Railways*

Steam to the Bank

Above: Ever since regular electric passenger trains to Addison Road (now Kensington Olympia) were withdrawn during the war, special trains have been run during weekday mornings and evenings for the benefit of staff from the National Savings Bank and other offices nearby. The trains remained steam-hauled until the very end of Southern steam in July, 1967, and were certainly the last steam-hauled suburban trains in London. Here, on June 29, 1967, just a few days before its final demise, BR standard class 3 2—6—2T No 82019 waits patiently at Olympia for the right away with the 4.36pm train to Clapham Junction. [*John H. Bird*

Below: Motive power on the Bank 'Flyer' varied; here BR standard class 4 2—6—4T No 80085 approaches the Central Section platforms at Clapham Junction with an afternoon train from Olympia. The leading vehicle of the train is the experimental fibreglass-bodied surburban coach No S1000.

[*G. D. King*

Rails Across Mid-Wales

Right: The staccato exhaust of BR standard class 4 4—6—0 No 75002 echoes beneath an overbridge near Talerddig as it storms towards the summit with the 7.30am Pwllheli-Paddington through train on August 6, 1966.

[*W. Brian Alexander*

Below: Ivatt class 2 2—6—0 No 46505 canters away from Welshpool with the two-coach Shrewsbury portion of the 12.35pm Aberystwyth-Whitchurch train on July 22, 1963.

[*Brian Stephenson*

On a hot day in August, 1963, the crew of No 7821 *Ditcheat Manor* take a breather against the fence as their Oswestry-bound freight waits in the loop at Carno for the down 'Cambrian Coast Express' to pass in the charge of sister engine No 7819 *Hinton Manor.*

[*M. J. Fox*

A peculiarity of Llanbrynmair Station was the level crossing which divided the down platform. Here, 4—6—0 No 7828 *Odney Manor* restarts a train for Aberystwyth in August, 1963.

[*Andrew Muckley*

CAMBRIAN COAST
EXPRESS
7803

Right: In latter years, BR standard engines were much in evidence on the Cambrian lines. Here, class 4 2—6—4T No 80135 rolls into Machynlleth with the 4.00pm Shrewsbury-Aberystwyth stopping train on July 24, 1963.
[*Brian Stephenson*

Left: Ivatt class 2 2—6—0 No 46521 takes the now-closed Bala line at Morfa Mawddach with the 4.05pm Barmouth-Dolgellau on August 4, 1964.
[*M. Dunnett*

Below Left: Complete with train of chocolate-and-cream liveried rolling stock, immaculate 7800 class 4—6—0 No 7803 *Barcote Manor* accelerates away from Dovey Junction with the up 'Cambrian Coast Express' on May 25, 1961.
[*C. P. Walker*

Below: The line south from Aberystwyth towards Lampeter and Carmarthen is now closed completely at the northern end and the remainder is open only for freight. But both this and the line from Llandilo in the foreground were still open on August 29, 1963, when 7400 class 0—6—0PT No 7445 clattered past Abergwili Junction with a southbound freight.
[*Anthony Vickers*

Having climbed all the way from Bala Junction, 4300 class 2—6—0 No 6316 swings through the passing loop at Carneddwen with a through Manchester-Barmouth train on August 29, 1959, and begins the descent to Dolgellau.
[*E. Frangleton*

Speeding through Glan Llyn Halt on the wooded slopes alongside Lake Bala comes BR standard class 4 4—6—0 No 75004 with a through train for Barmouth on August 31, 1963.
[*Andrew Muckley*

Interlude at Penmaenpool: 5800 class 0—4—2T No 5801 and 2251 class 0—6—0 No 2234 rest between trips in the small two-road running shed alongside the main line on June 24, 1956.

[*R. E. Vincent*

With the road toll bridge in the background, 4300 class 2—6—0 No 7341 restarts a Barmouth-Ruabon train from Penmaenpool on June 8, 1960.

[*Derek Cross*

Rural scene on the Cambrian Coast line at Minffordd: BR standard class 3 2—6—2T No 82005 leaves its lightweight train standing on the main line as it shunts the yard on July 31, 1964.
[*M. Dunnett*

The tide is out as a 2251 class 0—6—0 rumbles across Barmouth Bridge on August 10, 1957, with a stopping train from Machynlleth to Pwllheli.
[*R. E. Vincent*

Along the Dovey estuary, 4300 class mogul No 6392 coasts into Penhelig Halt with the 3.45pm Machynlleth-Pwllheli on May 11, 1961.

[*J. R. Besley*

On September 6, 1962, BR standard class 3 2—6—2T No 82003 rolls a short freight for Barmouth away from Towyn.

[*P. H. Wells*

There can be no doubt that the BR standard class 9F 2—10—0s were powerful, robust locomotives capable of both freight and passenger work. But the author argues that it was the theory rather than the design which was at fault; by the time the BR standard engines appeared, mass dieselisation or electrification should have been adopted. Here, No 92071 heads an Annesley-Woodford freight south of Ashby Magna in December, 1964.
[*M. Mitchell*

Forward from Steam

W. T. THORNEWELL

About 1934 a decision was made on the London & North Eastern Railway which had far reaching effects at the time, which has affected policy to the present, and which will continue to affect the position of railways in this country for the foreseeable future. The decision was that of the LNER Chief Mechanical Engineer, H. N. Gresley, to depend on steam locomotives for the projected high speed trains with which the Company intended to mark the Silver Jubilee of the reign of King George V.

At the time of the Gresley decision there was, in fact, very little new on the British scene to acclaim in terms of locomotive achievement. Apart from the Great Western's star performances, and the LNER adoption of Churchward's far-reaching technology on the Gresley Pacifics, there was little to enthuse about. Beyond the already ageing Great Western Kings and Castles, and the earlier LNER Pacifics, the British locomotive fleet was generally in the doldrums, even allowing for the LMS Royal Scots and the Southern King Arthurs and Lord Nelsons. In design, all were approaching ten years old, if not more.

Throughout the world, changes were coming about in the field of railway traction; the principles of electric traction were firmly established, and more than ten years earlier, the North Eastern had proposed to electrify its 'race track' section of the East Coast main line, between Newcastle and York. But the plan was promptly shelved by the newly-formed LNER and, as far as really powerful traction units were concerned, the East Coast Route had to rely on the later Great

Sir Vincent Raven's impressive prototype express electric locomotive No 13 for the North Eastern Railway's proposed York-Newcastle overhead electrification, seen here at the Railway Centenary Celebrations of 1925.

[*F. R. Hebron*

Northern designs for top-link power for many years.

After the decision of the LNER Board to enter the sphere of high speed trains, Gresley was instructed to decide what should be done. As it turned out, he had brilliant ideas, brilliantly executed, with several fine services brought into being.

As recounted by that doyen of writers, Cecil J. Allen, the triumphs of the new Gresley A4 Class streamlined locomotives were endless, and outstripped by far what was being done elsewhere in Britain. Undoubtedly, the Grest Western engines were doing better than ever, and soon after this the LMS took its first positive steps forward, but with locomotives, rolling stock and speeds the LNER raced forward to set a cracking pace. The LMS, despite its ever growing fleet of competent, reliable locomotives being built by Stanier, never matched the breathtaking glamour of the LNER, although both the Great Western and the LMS could be said to have been generally better equipped. The LMS attempt to beat Gresley's A4s was rather an abortive affair, and although they claimed 114mph descending from Whitmore to Crewe, the story of it left a bad taste in the mouth of the dedicated men who devoted their professional lives to the high standards of railway safety.

Even on the LNER there were at the time many railwaymen, some still with us, who were not very happy at the spectacle of *Silver Fox* limping into King's Cross, having shed some of its gear along the track, or to hear of the later happening when *Mallard* had to be taken off its train at Peterborough. Again, despite the passenger growth brought by the high speed trains, there were many troubles for those who had to deal with the complicated working of freight trains caused by the 'flyers'. After all, for all but perhaps the Southern, freight was still the life blood.

Now, it must be remembered that before Gresley initiated the high speed trials with his A1 and A3 Pacifics between King's Cross and Leeds, and King's Cross and Newcastle, he had looked farther afield to Germany where, since 1932, the Reichsbahn had been running a high speed streamlined diesel express between Berlin and Hamburg. These were early years for high-speed diesel haulage, but nevertheless the train captured the imagination of many professional railwaymen and enthusiasts alike. Gresley was quoted an estimated journey time of 4 hours 17 minutes from King's Cross to Newcastle by the German builders for a similar type of unit as the one operating the Hamburg service. There seem to have been no enquiries as to what a more powerful unit could achieve in order to overcome the many obligatory speed restrictions, to tackle the moderate climb to Stoke Summit, and to maintain generally higher speeds elsewhere. So it seems that Gresley himself made the decision that steam it must be – and there can be no doubt that in the short run he succeeded.

It is interesting to speculate whether the time of 4 hours from King's Cross to Newcastle which he laid down was influenced by the Germans' estimate of a faster time with their existing diesels than he could obtain with his existing Pacifics.

All this time, the LMS was on balance behind the LNER in locomotive accomplishment, and it seemed that, despite the advent of William Stanier, the cautionary spirits of Captain Huish and Sir Richard Moon were still exerting an undue influence on the higher counsels at Euston. Solid and comfortable, reasonably fast in comparison, but nothing spectacular in the daily services was the established pattern on the LMS.

With the coming of World War II, the railways coped magnificently with a staggering increase in traffic with their existing steam locomotives. They were still recovering when, in 1948, came Nationalisation. Once more a decision had to be made; was the future standard to be steam, diesel or electric? Despite the North Eastern project of nearly thirty years before, the success of the Southern electrified system, the problems of maintaining the high-speed steam engines in tip-top condition, and the generally run-down state of the railways, steam once again won the day. The

Gresley's answer to the high-speed dilemma: streamlined A4 Pacific No 4489 *Dominion of Canada* hurries the down 'Flying Scotsman' through Finsbury Park in pre-war days.

[*Eric Treacy*

The pride of the pre-war Deutsche Reichsbahn: one of the 'Flying Hamburger' high speed diesel railcars waits at Berlin's Lehrter station before making its 142-minute dash to Hamburg.

trials on foreign metals of various designs hardly helped towards a clear decision, because it seemed that the attitude of mind of the individual drivers was the governing factor, something which most professional railwaymen already knew. Out of these deliberations, whose worthy objective was to produce really general purpose, go-anywhere locomotives with maximum utility, there emerged two very good new designs – the Britannia mixed traffic Pacific locomotives and the outstanding 9F 2–10–0 freight engines. The other Standard classes were really adaptations of LMS types, a tribute to Stanier and Ivatt.

In the early 'fifties it soon became obvious that the vast expense of the Standard engines, good though they were, was proving to be an error, for steadily the railway image became more and more tarnished as time went on. For various reasons the public, who now footed the bill, convinced themselves that there had been a sad decline in the standard of service, and there can be no doubt that the image of the 'dirty old steam train' was a major factor. Just as people disliked being cooped up in a long-distance bus, so they disliked sitting bolt upright in the LNER articulated sets. Even the relatively more comfortable trains of the London Midland and Western Regions were said to be slow in starting, pedestrian in progress, and quite uncertain. Of course the position was exaggerated, but railway managements ought not to have regarded this as an excuse to preserve the status quo, or to allow the rather defeatist attitude which took consolation from the more obvious exaggerations to prevail. Steam trains were basically thought of as pre-World War I, for the Gresley glamour touched only the few, and remained only in the minds of a relatively small number of enthusiasts.

Ironically, the travelling public began to base their criticisms of the steam services, on the Eastern Region at least, on a comparison with the Shenfield electric services introduced in 1949, which already were showing in passenger comfort and speed how superior they were to the finest timings of the steam era, even to the remarkable service put on by the Great Eastern 'jazz' in an earlier era. Except in the morning and evening peaks, when the public in their wisdom insist on travelling at the latest possible moment in breathless haste, the electric services provided by the Southern had shown a remarkable improvement so far as speed and comfort were concerned, and even in the overcrowded rush hours the timings were immensely quicker and the services more reliable.

Looking back to the inter-war period, we can now recognise with hindsight some tendencies which were given very little regard at the time. The Great Western Railway in the 1930s had a modest number of diesel-driven railcars, most being powered by AEC equipment. One service was from Oxford to Hereford via Worcester and my wife and I had an opportunity to sample this one at first hand. Although brought up in a vast family of railway servants, with every side of steam locomotive handling and management fully represented, we were both enthralled by this revelation of what rail travel could mean. It was far more interesting than conventional steam train travel and conversation with other passengers underlined this most clearly. The same thing happened when the LMS tried the rubber-tyred Michelin railcar and, later, the three-car diesel train on faster timings between St Pancras, Leicester & Nottingham. It worked some suburban trains and some of the semi-expresses so necessary on the Midland line, with its large number of sizeable towns en route. These trains were very popular, and there was great regret among public and railwaymen alike when the diesel set was taken out of service 'because of the war'.

The so-called 'romance of steam' surely emanates from the fact that the steam engine can be seen 'coming to grips' with its load under adverse conditions, whereas there is very little evidence of the 'titanic struggle' with a diesel, and really none at all with an electric locomotive. Such was the attraction that the steam engine lobby tended to play down the deficiencies of steam and highlight the faults of rival forms of motive power. For example, few would dispute the relative inefficiency of the steam locomotive compared with the diesel or electric locomotive, but this was played down because coal is an indigenous fuel whereas oil has to be imported. Somehow, probably as a result of pressure from the powerful oil lobbies, Britain's growing network of modern, high capacity electricity power stations, many of which use coal, have been consistently ignored.

One thing seems quite certain: the intensive

Despite the predominance of steam between the wars, all four of the major railway companies experimented with other forms of traction. Here, an Armstrong-Whitworth two-coach railcar undergoes trials on the LNER in May, 1934.

Paradoxically, the GWR, who would have nothing whatsoever to do with electrification, were probably more amenable to diesel railcars than their northern brethren, and many of these handsome vehicles remained in traffic well into BR days. This AEC diesel twin, Nos 35 and 36, seated 184 passengers when marshalled with a GW standard corridor coach and provided a buffet service. [*AEC*

The crew of GWR 4300 class 2—6—0 No 6378 look somewhat startled as, looking more like an escaped road motor coach than a rail-borne vehicle, the Michelin pneumatic-tyred railcar accelerates away from Reading amidst a cloud of exhaust.

[*M. W. Earley*

steam locomotive construction programme did not do away with the difficulties that bedevilled British Railways in their early years. After the end of the war, in 1945, a considerable apathy was apparent everywhere. My experience as a railwayman showed that on many occasions, although steam engines were available, there were staff shortages, especially among the young men required to supplement the ranks of locomotive firemen, and as a result there were a lot of cancellations. Meanwhile, the LMS shunting diesels had shown that they could haul a steam engine and its train out of difficulty, with no fuss or photogenic clouds of smoke and steam, and with only one man on the footplate, which helped to overcome the shortage of young men prepared to immerse themselves in coal dust and dirt. These considerations cannot be elegantly dismissed, because it was these attitudes and antipathies which so often brought minor stoppages to the railways and constantly delayed the running of the railway in practical terms.

Today, few would doubt that the train services provided for both passenger and freight are much swifter than they ever were while steam reigned supreme, because the new forms of power are more capable of providing what is required. We know from the writings of the leading railway authors how often, when timings were tightened in steam days, they were maintained only with some difficulty. Yet today timings over many lines are quicker than they have ever been, despite additional stops. BR are beginning to realise that the public do not wish to change at junctions just to suit the convenience of the railway operating people. They want to avoid as much of this as possible and travel direct from commencing point to destination without changing, just as they would in a private car. Diesel and electric traction has enabled this to be done. For example, the cries of 'Paddington only' which used to be such a proud boast of the Great Western are now few, and as a result the service to the public is infinitely better. The Midland line out of St Pancras always did a lot of the short distance running, town to town, but now that steam has disappeared the whole service is far quicker, with still a fair number of non-stop trains over the St Pancras to Leicester distance.

The advent of electricity has revolutionised the services out of Euston where for the first time there is now an intensive service of semi-fasts to Birmingham – and this on a line which prided itself on long non-stop runs. Even by semi-fast, the end-to-end timings are little inferior to those of the non-stops of 40 years ago.

The experimental Fell diesel-mechanical 4—4—4—4 No 10100 at Derby in 1955. Built as a 4—8—4, the centre rods were subsequently removed to provide two separate sets of four-coupled driving wheels.

[P. H. Groom

One of the immediate results of Nationalisation in January, 1948, was the Locomotive Exchanges of the following summer. Although providing much interest in data (especially for the railway enthusiast!), they did no more than prove what many railwaymen had long suspected – that, given reasonably efficient locomotives, much depended on the efficiency and attitude of mind of the crew. Here, SR West Country class light Pacific No 34005 *Barnstaple* waits to depart from St Pancras with the 10.15am express to Manchester on June 16, 1948.

In steam days stops at stations were to be avoided by any possible means short of providing no service, and documents were produced in railway offices to show how much it cost to slow down, stop and re-start. One argument against intermediate stops of expresses was the relatively slow recovery of speed again. In this connection, it was fascinating to watch the performance of the experimental Fell diesel which ran for some time on the 12.05 from Derby to London, a typical semi-fast on the Midland. The acceleration was remarkable, and with this locomotive on the front it was common for the train to stand waiting for time, often several minutes, at intermediate stations. This was in marked contrast to what usually happened when a Stanier 5 was in charge.

Although in justice to our railways it must always be conceded that many allegations of dirty coaching stock often arise from the activities of the litter-happy public, there is also no doubt that modern forms of motive power do not give rise to so much grime in coaches as in the steam days.

So three fateful decisions were made which have subsequently adversely affected the position of our railways, and assisted the drift to road transport. Soon after the grouping in 1923 the North Eastern electrification project was cancelled; about 1934 Gresley opted for steam, not even giving, so far as we know, an opportunity to the Germans to demonstrate their 'Flying Hamburger' express (remember Churchward and the de Glehn compounds), and in 1948 a decision was made to standardise on steam, a most short lived and expensive palliative, despite the very fine 'Britannias'.

If the North Eastern electrification scheme had gone ahead there would undoubtedly have been difficulties at first, as there is with any new form of motive power, but as a result the British Railway system would have been nearly 40 years ahead in providing the sort of service that the public wants. Even in recent times, after over 100 years of experience, some new types of steam engine have given considerable trouble.

If Gresley had not been so firmly for steam express power, and had considered importing a German power unit with even the elementary suggestion of a more powerful engine, it is quite possible that it would not have been necessary to build a super-Pacific for the King's Cross–Newcastle run. The diesel would most probably have gone well below the much-lauded four hours of steam.

By 1950 there were already main line diesels in service on the LMR and the SR. There was ample evidence throughout the world that diesel and electric units were efficient and economical if used correctly. The decision to rely on steam was a mistake and a vast amount of money was spent with a short life and poor return. There is a lot of evidence to support the view that, despite the ageing life of the British steam engine fleet, many classes were fit for several more years of life, as witnessed by the performances that some put up late in the day when properly serviced. It was not the machines that suddenly became of little use, but other related factors that affected their reliability and economics. How could the construction of large numbers of new steam engines clear up the main problems, which were concerned with people and not machines. At a time when diesels were in general use I, on one occasion, came down Stoke Bank at 100mph on the racing stretch, behind an A3 Pacific. What was required in 1948 was an effort to use effectively the steam engines, which were as efficient as they had ever been, while conversion to more modern forms of motive power went ahead.

In 1923 we lost 40 years, in 1934 we lost 25 years, and in 1948 we lost at least another 10 years. Was romantic steam worth all that? Instead of being leaders we have become followers on the 'traffic' side of the railway business, although in the service departments we remain very much in the van.

There is no denying that the steam engine did us very well, and in the post-war years their performances were probably better than circumstances would lead us to expect. They were, however, already the symbols of a past age and not at all to the liking of most of the public and a majority of the railway staff, very few of whom enjoyed the flood of derogatory remarks that came their way.

In Britain we are still far from making full use of diesel and electric locomotive power. We seem once again to be pursuing a 'small engine' policy. Apart from the Deltics, there are still no diesels on BR of over 3000hp, and even the new 'super AL6' design for the extension of the West Coast electrification over Shap to Scotland would appear to be puny alongside some of the existing machines on the Continent. We have lost the lead; we must now learn the lessons of the past fifty years and regain the initiative.

After World War II, the LMS designed and built two English Electric powered main line 1,600 hp diesel-electric locomotives for evaluation, and soon after the Southern Railway ordered three similarly-powered prototypes. Although the initial decision went against dieselisation in favour of new steam engines, both the LMS and SR prototypes gave many years of useful service, and several aspects of their designs were incorporated in the first generation of BR Diesels. In this view, the second of the LMS 'twins', No 10001, hurries an Edge Hill-Willesden fitted freight up the North Western main line south of Berkhamsted.
[*E. D. Bruton*

The Little Railways of England

Right: Saved from extinction by a syndicate of enthusiasts, the 15in gauge Romney, Hythe and Dymchurch Railway still runs every day throughout the summer months. On May 17, 1970, No 7 *Typhoon* was taking water at New Romney before departing for Dungeness while, in the background, No 1 *Green Goddess* prepared to depart in the opposite direction with a train for Hythe.

[*D. L. Percival*

Below: The other popular enthusiast-supported 15in gauge line in England is 'the Ratty', the Ravenglass and Eskdale line in the Lake District. The R & ER's newest acquisition, 2—8—2 No 9 *River Mite*, heads the crowded 14.40 Ravenglass-Dalegarth near Beckfoot on June 8, 1969.

[*P. Silverwood*

Right: Leighton Buzzard Light Railway de Winton vertical-boilered 0—4—0 *Chaloner* rests at Leedon Loop prior to running round and re-attaching the brake truck, seen in the distance, to the back of the train.

[*P. H. Groom*

Left: Kerr Stuart 0—4—0ST *Pixie* waits in Leedon Loop on the Leighton Buzzard Light Railway before returning to Pages Park on July 25, 1970. *Pixie* was built in 1922 and spent most of her working life with the Devon County Council.

[*D. L. Percival*

Below Left: Between the trees on the then newly-opened Knebworth Country Park Railway comes Hunslet 0—4—0ST No 1 in August, 1971. Built in 1922 as Works No 1429, No 1 worked for many years in North Wales on the Dinorwic Quarry Railway.

[*P. R. Foster*

Below: Less intrepid visitors to Southend can traverse its lengthy pier on the comfortable pier electric railway. Here, a seven-car train of modern four-wheelers rumbles out towards the Pier Head in June, 1967.

[*G. R. Mortimer*

The Groudle Glen Railway on the Isle of Man lay inactive for many years before it was re-opened for summer visitors about a decade ago. Looking somewhat weathered, but steaming happily, 2—4—0T *Polar Bear* waits at the seaward terminus for homeward bound passengers on July 7, 1961.
[*L. Nicolson*

A little later, on a wet day in August, 1961, *Polar Bear* was fighting for adhesion on a particularly steeply-graded and sharply-curved section of line where the railway leaves the woods of the Glen and heads for the nearby cove.

Alderney's Railway

MICHAEL BRYAN

If asked, most railway enthusiasts would tell you that there are no railways on the Channel Islands. They would be wrong. Tucked away on Alderney is a 2½ mile long standard gauge line operated by the Department of the Environment. It is worked as required to bring granite from quarries in the north east of the island down to the harbour to repair the breakwater which was built in mid-Victorian days as part of a grand design to strengthen the island defences and which now needs frequent repair and attention. The breakwater extends for about 1000 yards into Braye Bay from Fort Grosnez on the north side of the island and must be one of the most exposed maritime structures in Europe.

The railway in its present form dates from 1950, the previous line having suffered during the German occupation of the island in the War. It has flat-bottom 60 or 80lb rail on concrete sleepers throughout, except on the breakwater, which carries 120lb rail. It begins at Mannez quarry, near the north-eastern tip of the island, and runs south-westwards through open country past Fort Albert to a point near Newtown, on the edge of St Anne's, the capital and only town of Alderney. There it turns north-west following the edge of Braye Bay, until it reaches the old harbour, and runs on to the breakwater. There is a run-round loop at the quarry and another near the landward end of the breakwater, together with a short spur into the engine shed. The ruling gradient is 1 in 130 and there are six ungated crossings.

The rolling stock of the line consists of 12 tippler wagons and one locomotive, a Ruston 88 DS 20-ton, four-wheel 88hp diesel, named Molly II. It was supplied in 1958 to replace the original Molly, a four-wheel Sentinel steam locomotive which even today is still affectionately remembered by islanders, though it did sometimes set fire to the countryside in dry summers! Like the Sentinel, the diesel carries a lifebelt, a reminder of the hazards of operation on the breakwater. A warning siren adds another nautical touch. Because it was too heavy for any Alderney crane to lift, Molly II was delivered in parts and was assembled on the island.

The sole motive power on the Department of the Environment's quarry railway on Alderney is this Ruston & Hornsby 0—4—0 diesel *Molly 2*. Note the substantial engine shed, only built in 1958, and the lifebelt on the rear of the cab.

[*DOE*

The 'Cambridge Buffet Express'

D. L. PERCIVAL

During the quarter of a century since Nationalisation, most named expresses have undergone a transition from steam to diesel power. Unlike most, however, the 'Cambridge Buffet Express' has not enjoyed a dramatic acceleration—in any case, the word 'express' is somewhat misleading. At present, in fact, its title is unofficial, since it disappeared from the timetable in 1964, but it is still known as 'the Buffet'.

The 'Cambridge Buffet Express' is not an express in the usual sense of the word, but a series of semi-fast trains running between King's Cross and Cambridge several times a day, including Sundays since May 1971. Its history goes back to the early 'thirties, when the London & North Eastern Railway decided to improve the train service between London and Cambridge in an attempt to secure more passenger traffic. The ex-Great Eastern route to Liverpool Street was congested at the London end, so the slightly longer 58-mile route via Hitchin to King's Cross was chosen, and five trains daily in each direction were inaugurated in May 1932. The trains made intermediate stops at Welwyn Garden City and Letchworth—as well as Hitchin, where they left the ex-Great Northern main line—hence the appropriate (but cumbersome) title 'Garden Cities and Cambridge Buffet Express' which was disregarded by Cambridge undergraduates in favour of 'the Beer Trains'. The timings were 82 minutes down and 77 minutes up, shortened to 75 down and 72 up in 1933, and the trains were hauled by Great Northern Large Atlantics, Great Eastern B12 4-6-0s and Claud Hamilton 4-4-0s, and LNER B17 4-6-0s. Other classes appeared from time to time, including Great Central C4 Atlantics.

Initially, the trains were three-coach formations, including a buffet car, and an innovation was the provision of armrests in the third class compartments. Their popularity quickly grew, and so did they—to six coaches, strengthened to nine or ten at busy times. In 1939, departures from King's Cross on Mondays to Fridays were 9.35, 12.40, 2.10, 8.10 and 11.40; up trains left Cambridge at 9.25, 12.30, 3.30, 5.25 and 10.10.

Discontinued during the war, the trains were restored on December 6, 1948, with the simpler title 'Cambridge Buffet Express'. Four trains ran in each direction, down at 9.35, 12.5, 2.25 and 8.30, and up arrivals at 10.57, 1.38, 4.47 and 6.52. Extra stops were made by some services at Baldock or Royston and, in addition, speed restrictions south of

Left: For some time quite regular performers on the 'Cambridge Buffet Express', the Thompson L1 2—6—4Ts worked a considerable number of other King's Cross outer suburban services as well, including the 11.21am King's Cross-Baldock, seen here crossing Woolmer Green viaduct in the charge of 67785 on August 20, 1956. [*R. M. Newland*

Above: The 12.50pm Cambridge-King's Cross nears journey's end as it hurries through Wood Green in the charge of a Brush class 31 on July 3, 1970. The leading vehicle of the train is the Cravens experimental open second of 1957, forerunner in many ways of the present BR Mk II stock. [*Michael Baker*

Hatfield and between Hitchin and Cambridge prevented a return to pre-war timings; the fastest was 88 minutes. In October 1950, the timetable was revised and departures became 9.5, 12.5, 2.5 and 8.5 from King's Cross, and 9.10, 12.10, 3.10 and 6.10 from Cambridge. The King's Cross outer suburban service at this time was operated in the main by modern steam power, and in the early 1950s the 'Buffets' were powered by B1s, Gresley B17s (notably the later 'Footballers') and the Thompson B2 rebuilds of Cambridge depot, while King's Cross and Hitchin depots used B1s on their duties.

During the next few years, I was able to observe the 'Buffets' being worked by many types of locomotive, some on a regular basis, and others as occasional visitors. 'Regulars' included LMS 'Black Five' 44911 and BR Standard Class 5 73071, which were allocated to King's Cross from February 1956 until June 1957 and three more Standards, 73157/8/9, allocated there for twelve months from October 1957. Another type which saw occasional use was the L1 2-6-4T, especially on Summer Saturdays when King's Cross shed had no B1 available. Some of that depot's outer suburban duties provided a Pacific, and one occasionally found its way into a 'Buffet' working, as did A1 60136 *Alcazar*, which worked the 12.5 up one August Saturday in 1957; by way of contrast, that day's 3.15 up was powered by L1 67791!

The 'Buffets' powered by Cambridge shed saw a variety of motive power from East Anglian depots, mainly B1s and B17s of course, but also K1 and K3 2-6-0s. Cambridge's own B12s were also used on occasions; 61575/6 were seen early in 1957, while 61549/64/80 appeared in the summer of 1958, in each case on the 3.15 up. The return working of the 3.15's locomotive was the

A down combined Cambridge and Peterborough train passes New Barnet on August 16, 1956, in the charge of B1 class 4—6—0 No 61327 and L1 class 2—6—4T No 67768.

5.52 to Cambridge and Peterborough, on which it was usually piloted to Hitchin (where the 11-coach train divided) by the B1 off an afternoon stopping train from Peterborough. When the Cambridge engine was a B12, the two 4-6-0s made an interesting pair! Probably the last occasion when a B12 worked the 'Buffet' was on January 23, 1959, when 61580 hauled the 7.55 down. No mention can be made of the 3.15 up without recalling that it was the regular working of the Cambridge Royal Engine, 61671 *Royal Sovereign*. Always immaculately turned out, this B2 powered the train for many years until a couple of months before it was withdrawn in September 1958.

By that time, the first diesel locomotive had already appeared, as Hornsey's English Electric Type 4s, D201/6-9, had arrived during the spring and summer. The first diesel-powered 'Buffet' was probably the 11.15 up, hauled by D201 on May 13, and as the new locomotives arrived, each spent a few days on a similar duty before taking up main-line work.

In final steam days, Cambridge locomotives handled four of the trains, King's Cross powered the 11.15 up and 12.25 and 2.16 down, while a Hitchin B1 worked the 9.25 down. During the winter of 1958/9, which was the last of the 'steam' timetables, the four trains in each direction left King's Cross at 9.25, 12.25, 2.16 and 7.55, and Cambridge at 9.15, 11.15, 3.15 and 6.15. The fastest timings were held by those which called only at Welwyn, Hitchin and Letchworth—the 11.15 up and 2.16 down (80 minutes) and the 3.15 up (81 minutes). The others also called at Royston, and the 7.55 called at Baldock as well, while the 9.25 down missed Royston but called at Stevenage and Baldock.

At the beginning of February 1959, when the first stage of outer suburban dieselisation began, the 9.25 down and 9.15, 11.15 and 3.15 up 'Buffets' were included in diagrams covered by BRCW Type 2s in the D5300–19 series. A King's Cross B1 powered the 6.15 up and the other three were handled by Cambridge locomotives. This changed when the second stage was instituted at the end of March, all 'Buffets' being rostered for diesel haulage from that time. However, this was by no means the end of steam, as numerous diesel failures during the next few months saw B1s and even L1s coming to the rescue on occasional workings. Probably the worst performers were the NBL Type 2s, D6100–9, which were delivered to Hornsey between the end of March and late May. These 1,000hp machines made heavy weather of the 'Buffets' but the trains were soon provided with another diesel type when the Summer 1959 timetable commenced in June. The new English Electric 'Baby Deltics' took over about a third of the outer suburban service, including four of the eight 'Buffets'. About this time, the first 'foreign' diesel appeared, when Stratford's D6116 came up with the 3.15 on June 18. Brush type 2s came into the picture from December 1959 onwards, and the BRCW and NBL Type 2s were transferred away in the following year.

With the Summer 1959 timetable, the Stevenage stop was instituted, reflecting the growth of this third 'new town' on the route. As an experiment, one of the 'Buffet' sets was used on a late morning service to Royston, returning in the early afternoon, and the other formed a 5.26 evening 'local' to Royston (on which its crowded buffet car was in use as far as Hitchin) and returned to King's Cross later in the evening. In the following September the Royston trains were extended to Cambridge and, since the 5.26 (and its successors) was un-named, there were five down and six up 'Cambridge Buffet Expresses'. In September 1960, the 3.5 down was extended to Ely, returning from there at 5.33 and continuing as the 5.57 from Cambridge; this arrangement lasted until April 1966.

During most of the BR period, the two 'Buffet' sets were seven coach formations (sometimes eight), including an LNER buffet car—usually of Gresley design, although Thompson 1947 'Flying Scotsman' cars E1705E and E1706E have also appeared in one of the formations since the mid-1960s. In September 1962, the other set had its Gresley buffet replaced by a BR Standard miniature buffet car; its workings lost their official title in the Summer 1963 timetable, but the name was restored in September of that year—only to be removed again when the name 'Cambridge Buffet Express' lost its official status in the following May. Needless to say, any working which was un-named for any reason still sported carriage roofboards, as was the case for a long time after May 1964!

Further changes in motive power had occurred in the early 'sixties. Diesel 'substitutes' appeared in the shape of English Electric Type 1s in 1960; D5094, the forerunner of the one-time Finsbury Park Fleet of BR/Sulzer Type 2s (which were never regular performers on the Cambridge run) made trial runs in November of that year; and the Brush prototype D0280 (now 1200) *Falcon* put in a couple of appearances

Brush class 31 No 5596 accelerates away from Gasworks Tunnel with the 4.35pm King's Cross-Cambridge on May 9, 1970.
[*J. H. Cooper-Smith*

in October and November 1961, at the beginning of its stay on the Eastern Region. The last occasions when steam haulage was seen included the use of March K1 62066 in January 1960, Leicester Standard Class 4 75061 in October 1960, and a B1 in January 1963. Baby Deltics disappeared from the scene during 1962/3, but reappeared after modification in July 1964; the first to return was D5904, which on its third day back worked a diagram which included four of the 'Buffets'.

Brush Type 4s were by now regularly working these trains, and BR/Sulzer Type 4s and Deltics were used from time to time. As in steam days, there were occasional visitors—one of the early Brush Type 2s, D5502, powered the 5.30 Ely-King's Cross on the snow-disrupted New Year's Day of 1962; the experimental orange-liveried D5579 came up with the 9.15 one day in April 1964; and Stratford English Electric Type 3s worked the same train once or twice in the autumn of 1965. The last occasion when an English Electric Type 1 worked a 'Buffet' was on April 12, 1966, when D8027 replaced a failed Baby Deltic on an up early morning Baldock train and remained in the diagram to power the 9.04 down; the Type 1s were transferred away from Finsbury Park a few days later. Changes in the carriage workings in this period resulted in one set forming the 6.50 am King's Cross-Cambridge, which was hauled by a Brush Type 4 and called at all stations except Harringay and Hornsey! Unusual locomotive workings occurred in August and September 1966, when the 17.40 up 'Buffet' was powered by a BR/Sulzer Type 2 from Ipswich depot on two occasions.

As far as I am aware, the only time that the 'Buffets' were double-headed by design was during this period, when a pair of Baby Deltics powered the 15.34 down and 17.40 up on

Withdrawn from traffic for some time after recurrent engine failures, the English Electric 'Baby Deltics' were returned to traffic in 1964 with new engines, four-character headcode panels and the distinctive 'Big Deltic' two-tone livery. Thus modified, D5904 heads a Cambridge buffet express through Hatfield in the mid-sixties. [*Eric Treacy*

Even top-link locomotives appeared on Hitchin-Cambridge line trains between turns on the East Coast main line. On one such occasion, on August 28, 1957, A4 Pacific No 60028 *Walter K. Whigham* takes the Hitchin line at Shepreth Branch Junction with the 10.35am Cambridge-Hitchin.

[*J. A. Coiley*

several occasions. Oddly enough, a Brush Type 2/Brush Type 4 pairing was also seen twice on another 'Buffet' working during September. A second prototype to appear was English Electric's DP2, which during the first fortnight of October 1966 found regular employment on the 17.26 down and 20.15 up trains.

In recent years, there have been no additional diesel types on the 'Buffet', although locomotives from far-afield depots have appeared, including some of the LMR Stoke Division Brush Type 4s which find their way to King's Cross on Freightliner trains.

The past 25 years have seen a revolution in our railway system, but there are still links with the past. As far as the 'Buffet' is concerned, at the time of writing there is still a Gresley buffet car in one of the two sets and the schedules are only slightly faster than in the final days of steam—81 or 82 minutes is normal, and the best are a 77 minute Sunday timing and the 78 minute timing of one of the weekday trains. Locomotive workings, of course, are more varied when one considers the depots represented. In steam days, a Haymarket locomotive on the 'Cambridge Buffet Express' was a rare event indeed, and as for locomotives from the Western Region . . . !

But to those who remember the days before diesels took over, a visiting Stratford Class 31 arriving at King's Cross with a 'Buffet' is not the same as a Stratford B17. The old regulars like *Blickling*, *Lambton Castle* and *Huddersfield Town* were better than an anonymous LMR Class 47. And to compare the sight of even an ex-works Class 31 with that of the immaculate *Royal Sovereign* is unthinkable!

North of Inverness

Above: With snow-dusted mountains as a back-cloth, Birmingham RCW class 26 No 5335 skirts the Moray Firth near Inverness with a short freight from Kyle of Lochalsh on the last day of April, 1971.
[*J. H. Cooper-Smith*

Below: A southbound goods in the charge of ex-Caledonian Railway 4—4—0 No 54445 prepares to take the avoiding line at Inverness in July, 1951.

Right: BR/Sulzer class 24 No D5123, complete with twin headlights, passes Muir of Ord with a freight from Wick on April 30, 1971.
[*J. H. Cooper-Smith*

BR/Sulzer class 24 No D5130 pauses at the spacious down platform at Dingwall with the 10.30am Inverness-Wick on September 4, 1968.
[D. A. Bosomworth

Ex-Caledonian Railway '812' class 0—6—0 No 57594 blackens the sky at Dingwall as it pulls away from the up yard on July 23, 1959 with a heavy freight for Inverness and the south.
[Peter Tatlow

Birmingham RCW class 26 No 5336 curves past Muir of Ord with the 17.00 Inverness-Wick on April 30, 1971.

[J. H. Cooper-Smith

Pannier far from home: sent north to replace ageing Scottish sisters, ex-GW 1600 class 0—6—0PT No 1649 shunts the yard at Dingwall on August 21, 1961.

[J. C. Haydon

Stanier 'Black 5' 4—6—0 No 44991 restarts the 8.35am Wick-Inverness train from Tain on July 23, 1959.

[Peter Tatlow

The 10.30am Inverness-Wick and Thurso passenger and mail train rolls into Lairg behind Birmingham RCW Sulzer class 26 No D5319 on May 26, 1965. Note the Royal Mail connecting bus on the up platform to the extreme left.

[N. A. Machell

With the loco shed and wild mountain slopes in the background, Stanier class 5 4—6—0 No 44718 eases the morning Wick-Inverness train into the up platform at Helmsdale on September 22, 1954.

[L. King

BR standard class 2 2—6—0 No 78052 stands at The Mound with a train for Dornoch awaiting the arrival of the morning train from Wick to the south on May 29, 1957. In the background, an ex-GWR 1600 class 0—6—0PT waits to attach a restaurant car to the rear of the same train.

[J. Spencer Gilks

Busy scene at Achnasheen: BR/Sulzer class 24 No D5120 waits in the down platform with the 10.30 Inverness-Kyle of Lochalsh while another member of the same class brings the 10.57 Kyle of Lochalsh-Inverness into the passing loop.
[David Birch

Ex-Highland Railway class 4P 4—6—0 No 54767 *Clan Mackinnon* waits to depart from the yard at Kyle of Lochalsh with an up cattle train on September 27, 1948.
[C. C. B. Herbert

Birmingham RCW class 26 No D5336 follows the shores of Loch Carron near Strome Ferry with an Inverness-Kyle of Lochalsh train on July 17, 1971.
[*Derek Cross*

Barry

'30772'

Above: One in deceptively-modern British Rail blue, the other still in locomotive green, original North British Warship class diesel hydraulic locomotives Nos D600 *Active* and D601 *Ark Royal* await the same fate as the steam locomotives, beyond, they were intended to replace. [*P. R. Foster*

Below: The setting sun catches a group of ex-GW locomotives in the twilight of their lives. The cast metal number plate of 5100 class 2—6—2T No 5199 has long since been removed, and the boiler cladding of the tenderless 2800 2—8—0 beyond has been torn open. But all is not yet lost: the 5100 in the left distance has been repainted prior to removal for preservation, and the cylinders of the locomotive in the right foreground carry the hopeful message "Reserved". [*A. P. Higgins*

Steam is dead.
Nowhere can this be said
With more certainty than here, where
Almost two hundred steamers await their
Fate.

The largest collection of steam engines in the land
Since the heydays of Stratford, Willesden, York, stand
Buffer to buffer, nose to tail,
Cold and grey. Once giants of the rail
Were they—

Speeding to the Strong country
Or trundling over the S & D;
Working the humblest freights or crack
Expresses – 'Atlantic Coast', 'Bristolian' – there and back
They ran.

Western, Southern, LMS,
LNER, Standards – yes –
And diesels too
(Even one repainted blue!)
Lie dead

In this graveyard of steam. But, strange,
There is no rivalry – a change
From the days when talk was of 'King' versus 'Navy',
"28" or "8 Freight", 'Jub' against 'Castle', 'Bongo' v 'Mickey'!
Now they are equal.

More here than can be found at any preserved line,
Not for them the bright livery and polished shine
Of their sisters. No blue, maroon or apple green
In this society, just an overall scheme
Of grime and rust.

Right: Ex-LMS Jubilee class 4—6—0 No 45699 *Galatea.*

Below: A forlorn vista of rusting ex-GWR, ex-SR and BR standard locomotives, seen from the tender of ex-GWR 6000 class 4—6—0 No 6024 *King Edward I.*

Nearly half are Swindon-built. Some have seen a decade pass
While waiting the torch, and weeds and grass
Have taken root on step and footplate;
Fortyfives and fiftyfives stand and await
The end of their lives.

Great Western numberplates have gone, and all
The identification is a painted scrawl
On cabside. Wandering round, railway enthusiast who never
Expected such a sight adds "steam for ever",
Chalked in white.

Bulleid Pacifics – rebuilds and 'flat tops' –
Many years and miles gone by since they last went through shops.
'Battle of Britains' – once so many, now so few – stand forlorn
With gaping holes from where proud names have been torn –
Manston *and* Tangmere.

Fowler, Stanier, Ivatt engines that will never more see Derby or Crewe,
Never again will pound the tracks they knew.
Black Fives and 8Fs – BR's last steam, the last of the breed –
Can be seen in this forgotten yard where grows the weed
In their shadows.

Left: Only weeds now thrive on the footplate of ex-SR S15 class 4—6—0 No 30841.

Below: 'Rebuilds and Flat Tops' await the same fate: West Country Class Pacifics 34101 *Hartland* and 34105 *Swanage* at rest.

Right: Where once the proud crest of Battle of Britain Pacific No 34067 *Tangmere* was displayed, there is now nothing but a gaping hole.

Below right: Fowler, Stanier and Ivatt – class 3F 0—6—0T No 47298, class 5F 2—6—0 42968 and class 2F 2—6—0 No 46447.

Above: 'Twelve-sixty four'. The lone example of ex-LNER motive power, chimney-less B1 class 4—6—0 No 61264, later Departmental No 29.

Below: 'The Duke'. With cylinders and motion removed for display in the Science Museum, the now-naked boiler of BR standard class 8 Pacific No 71000 *Duke of Gloucester* looks longer than ever.

North Eastern engines went elsewhere, but one found
Its way here after travelling around.
'Twelve-sixtyfour, sole representative of the LNER,
Stands in line after serving as stationary boiler –
As Departmental 29.

After less than twenty years, the Standard locos were doomed.
Almost every class is here – even 'the Duke' – and 9Fs that loomed
Out of the night on fish and freight. Class 4 tanks stand side by side
With consecutive numbers. Coincidence? Or was it fate they died
Together, one wonders.

Right: Set aside. Ex-GWR class 7800 4—6—0 No 7827 *Lydham Manor* has been saved from the scrap merchant's torch and is now at the Dart Valley Railway.

Below: Also saved from this grim fate are ex-LMS 4F 0—6—0 No 43924 and ex-SR class U mogul No 31618; both have since moved to pastures new.

Along with steam, the diesel also stands inactive.
What value now its fifty thousand tractive
Effort? Steam's successor on the rails –
But a heavy price is paid if it fails
To make the grade.

But wait! Preservationists have cast their eyes on some
Of the rusting hulks. For these there is a new life to come.
Set aside, towed away, carefully repaired and cleaned,
Comes the great day when they are steamed
Again.

Restored to their former glory, eventually
In some well-known centre or pleasant valley
They become a living memorial to the days long past.
Their new owners have realised their dream; it can be said at last:
"Steam is dead – long live steam!"

The Other Side of the Fence

E. J. ALYSON

Railways are a thing apart; people have free access to roads, and they know what is good and bad about them, but they have no idea what goes on in the private world of the railway, on the other side of the wire fence and the stern admonition 'Persons are warned not to trespass upon the Railway'. I was lucky. I was born into a railway family and have been on the 'other side' ever since. Just as railways are a mystery to most, so railwaymen appear to be a race apart – often working unimaginable hours and always concerned with the system. Often they work alone, with no-one to turn to in a crisis. I am sure it is because they work largely on their own initiative, and because they feel that they are misunderstood by the public, that many incidents go unremarked. Some are serious, some are sad, others are, in retrospect, amusing. But all deserve to be told, because they are part of the social history of railways.

My experience of railwaymen at work has mostly been on the South Western lines of the Southern. Here, for many years, steam and electric trains shared the same tracks. After the Portsmouth electrification in 1937, few steam trains deigned to stop between Waterloo and Woking. An exception was the 08.35 Waterloo – Bournemouth train, which called at Surbiton to pick up about 08.53. It was always quite heavily loaded, and in latter years was usually in the charge of a rebuilt Bulleid Pacific, either a West Country or a Merchant Navy. Now, it had to turn onto the down local line at Surbiton, there being no platform on the down through, and it was usually immediately turned back onto the through line at the end of the platform. One morning, it was a few minutes late. The colour light at the end of the platform duly cleared as the train approached, three white lights above the green aspect indicating that the route was set, as usual, back onto the down through. On this particular morning, perhaps keen to regain time, the driver approached rather more enthusiastically than usual and, despite a sharp brake application, overshot the platform and came to a stand with his cab just beyond the signal which, because the overlap here was very short, unbeknown to him reverted to danger. An amusing situation therefore arose; the crew, having busied themselves around the locomotive for a few moments, peered back out of the cab awaiting the 'right away'. The station staff, meanwhile, having finished their platform work, looked up to see the platform starter at danger and, assuming that there was some delay, merely stood about in groups, talking. Over in the box, the signalman was busy coping with the tail end of the morning rush hour on the up lines and did not notice that, although the lever remained pulled, the starter had tripped back to danger.

Minutes ticked by. Still nothing happened. The fireman remarked to the driver that it was taking a long time to unload the few sacks of mail from the utility van, out of sight round the curve in the platform at the back of the train. At length the driver sent his mate to investigate. Climbing down from the engine, he walked up the ramp and, without glancing up at the signal, walked the length of the train to enquire as to the cause of the delay. Still nobody on the platform twigged. Then the telephone rang. The signalman had spotted that the signal had reverted to danger and, seeing the lack of intended movement, had guessed what had happened. Soon all was revealed, a yellow flag was thrust from the window of the box, and the train was on its way. But not before twenty minutes had been lost. It would be interesting to know how the delay was accounted for!

Thinking of Surbiton reminds me of another occasion when I was travelling over the nearby branch to Hampton Court. It was a cold, foggy late Autumn morning, but all went well until we were brought to a stand by an adverse signal on the lofty brick viaduct approach to the flyover at Hampton Court Junction. To the left and right, and beneath us obscuring the ground, swirled the fog. The motorman gave several determined blasts on his whistle, but the semaphore remained resolutely at danger. The signal carried a white diamond to indicate that the line was track circuited, but there was no 'phone. Our motorman had just reluctantly decided that he would have to leave the warmth of his cab and grope his way to the box when out of the mist appeared one of the signalmen from the busy Hampton Court Junction box below us. Apparently, a stairway is provided from the main line up to the flyover.

'Block failure', he announced, 'but you're clear through to Hampton Court. When you get there, blow up to let him know.' With a short blast of acknowledgement on the whistle, we set off. Now, I assumed that, having called at Thames Ditton, we would draw forward to the Hampton Court down outer home which, because the line is on a falling gradient here, is some distance in rear of the box and its adjacent level crossing. But no. Our motorman took his message a little too literally and, trundling past the fog-enshrouded home at danger, brought his train gently to a stand only a few yards away from the level crossing gates, which were still open to the road and across which traffic was obliviously passing. The driver gave two long blasts on his whistle, and I can see to this day the look of amazement on the face of the signalman as he peered out of the box at this train which had crept up on him out of the gloom so completely unannounced!

Hampton Court was a jolly place; on at least two occasions they drove electric trains out of the sidings when the points weren't set, with the amusing but expensive result that the train instead went through the trap points, demolished the buffer stop and various items of signalling equipment and then took to the road alongside the level crossing. On one occasion they all but demolished the signalbox as well!

Level crossings can be quite a headache for signalmen. In some boxes on the Southern they have so much trouble with irate and impatient motorists coming up to the box and demanding to know why they shouldn't be given precedence that the signalmen habitually lock the door.

Level crossings can also be a snare for the unwary. Immediately after the last war, before the Isle of Wight railway system was heavily truncated in the 1950's, the Ventnor West branch was worked on the one-engine-in-steam principle, usually with a Brighton 'Terrier' and a push-pull coach. This meant that the signalman at Merstone, the junction with the Sandown–Newport line, had no advance warning of the approach of the returning branch train, although of course he knew what time it was due. The practice was for the driver of the branch train to give a blast or two on his whistle as he approached from Godshill. The signalman would then close the level crossing gates and, if the line was clear, pull off the home signal which, because it also protected the junction, was situated some little way along the branch, around the corner in a cutting and out of sight of the box.

On the occasion I have in mind, the inevitable happened; the driver whistled as usual, the signalman closed the gates and pulled off, the driver gave a toot of acknowledgement – and then for some inexplicable reason, the signalman returned the signal to danger and absentmindedly opened the gates again! But of course the driver of the branch train had passed the home signal before it returned to danger, and he came cantering round the corner – straight through the gates!

Signalmen are an interesting breed of men. Most spend all their working hours alone in the box, often at night and sometimes in very remote and unfriendly locations. I once met a signalman who was a keen builder of model locomotives, but whose remote box was not connected to the mains electricity supply. Undaunted, he would, in slack hours, connect his small soldering iron to the low voltage batteries in the box. The lineman was always complaining about the number of failures on the equipment they supplied, but to my knowledge he never discovered the illicit uses to which his batteries were put in the small hours. Eventually, the signalman was posted elsewhere and miraculously the equipment gave no more trouble!

Another signalman friend was a keen railway photographer and one night, looking through the notices, he discovered that an enthusiasts' special, headed by a locomotive he particularly wanted to photograph, was due to pass his box the following weekend. But he was on duty, so how could he get out to photograph it? His mate was not available to cover for him. Eventually he hit on a plan. When the special was offered, he accepted it and offered it on to the next box, but he did not pull off. As the train came snorting into view, whistle protesting at the adverse signals, he rushed out onto the box verandah, took a couple of shots, and then tore back inside to pull off before the train came finally to a stand. The day was fine and the angle perfect. As soon as he booked off, he rushed home to get the film developed and prints ready to send off hopefully to the railway enthusiast press. Hours later, he was admiring the big glossy prints and congratulating himself on the arrangement when, horror of horrors, he recognised a face among the enthusiasts peering from the first coach of the train that sent a shiver down his spine. There, glaring at him from the third window of the first carriage was none other than his Area Inspector. Needless to say, the pictures did not appear and that particular method of railway photography was not repeated!

Area Inspectors are the bain of some signalmen's lives, but I am bound to say that those I have come across I have found to be strict, but fair. And that is how it should be. I remember that on one occasion I was accompanying an AI on business in a Sykes box on the South Western main line. The signalman was a man of great experience and he had a young lad with him who was training. The condition and operation of the box was immaculate (and it remained so almost to the day it was demolished after the introduction of colour light signalling). A light engine hurried past in the pouring rain and failed to activate the treadle which freed the Sykes Lock and Block instrument. The young lad was donning his coat before going down to kick the treadle when the older man stopped him and led him instead to a corner at the back of the box. He turned to look at the frame, and then stamped his foot smartly on the floor. The Sykes indicator flew from the locked to the free position. Before the AI could query this highly unconventional form of release, the old man was explaining that the box structure had shifted and sometimes fouled some of the equipment, causing it to stick. 'You should report that' declared the AI. The old man nodded. 'Your predecessor told my guvnor the self same thing when I was learning twenty five years back' he observed. No more was said!

Presently, there was a change of duty at the next box up the line. Obviously the message that the AI was around had not reached the man who had just come on duty, because he began to offer trains without calling attention. The old man was clearly embarrassed. If he accepted the unprefaced signals without query, he would be condoning the malpractice before his AI and a young trainee, yet if he continued to ignore the bells, the 13.50 to Portsmouth was going to be unnecessarily checked. The AI, realising his quandary, stepped out onto the verandah, ostensibly to light his pipe. He was not gone for more than two minutes, but this was enough to alert the man up the line of the situation.

The biggest headache of all railwaymen, however, is the awkward passenger. You get them every day, complaining about this, demanding to know that, and telling all and sundry to do the other. Most of the time they are just annoying and time-consuming, but just occasionally they are downright dangerous. On the Southern, many of the commuters behave like sheep; when Clapham A signalbox partially collapsed in the middle of the morning rush hour in the mid-sixties, the ensuing chaos was made infinitely worse by irresponsible passengers baling out of the trains where they stood. This meant that the power supply to many sections of conductor rail had to be cut off, and the attempts by railway staff to turn trains back and get a service working again were completely negated. But perhaps the best example of passenger idiocy is one which I witnessed myself. I was returning home on the 21.50 Waterloo–Portsmouth Harbour fast one winter night when, as we hurried through Walton-on-Thames, there was a flash, a loud report, and all the lights went out. To make matters worse, the emergency lighting system did not cut in, so the illuminated red warning panel at the rear of the train was also extinguished. Whether it was this, or the original flash and report, that attracted the attention of the Walton signalman I do not know, but evidently he sent 'stop and examine' to his mate at Weybridge, because the latter's down through line home signal returned to danger in our face as we came lurching to a standstill in the darkness of Weybridge cutting, a little way beyond Oatlands intermediate box, which was switched out. The driver lost no time in getting to a nearby signal head telephone to report the situation and establish via the Weybridge signalman whether or not the power supply had been cut off. Meanwhile, the Guard went to the rear of the train to fix his handlamp in position in lieu of the failed blind, and then began to search for the cause of the trouble.

Most passengers, including myself, remained seated, it being almost impossible to move very far in safety because of the inky darkness. But one traveller in my carriage, which was near the front of the train, became very agitated and kept jumping up from his seat, lowering the corridor window and demanding to know what was going on. The driver, walking back alongside the train from the telephone, assured him that everything was being done to get the train moving again, but the agitated passenger, who I could now see wore a bowler hat and sported an umbrella, became even more upset and began to exhort his fellow passengers to leave the train and walk along the line to Weybridge Station. No-one took much notice – a few people grunted disapproval, and two previously silent women opposite me began talking nervously.

Next, I heard the slam of a carriage door and the hesitant scrunch of uncertain feet on ballast. 'Where the hell are you going?' demanded an angry voice from outside. 'I'm a passenger and I'm fed up and I'm walking to Weybridge' came the reply. 'Well I'm the driver and I'm telling you to get back inside that train before you get yourself killed' responded the angry voice. The agitated passenger began to argue when, with a peremptory blast on its horn, an eight-car semi-fast to Alton clattered past at about 70mph on the adjacent down local line. Now, even railwaymen of vast experience do not stand so close to trains passing at speed unless they have to; the effect at night on an unsuspecting, somewhat neurotic passenger must have been devastating, for the red tail light of the passing train was still diminishing in the distance towards Weybridge when the carriage door was wrenched open, and the somewhat dishevelled and greatly abashed passenger clambered in and crept away down the corridor.

In another ten minutes, the source of the trouble was located, the faulty unit isolated, and the current, and therefore the lights, restored. We were soon under way again to Woking, where the erring Portsmouth unit was detached, and we finally departed about forty five minutes late. I suspect, however, that if it hadn't been for the timely passing of the Alton train, we should all have sat in Weybridge Cutting a good deal longer while the current was cut off to allow one selfish and misguided passenger to reach safety!

Railwaymen in general still have many things to learn about public relations. One is that most of the public are not fools. Another is that some of them are.

Locomotives in Disguise

J. A. LINES

A fancy dress ball or masquerade is always popular. In the one, familiar figures appear in unfamiliar garb, in the other the fun lies in guessing the identity of the person beneath the disguise.

Those with a taste for entertainment of that kind, and an interest in railways, can derive the same sort of pleasure in discovering well known locomotive types in less familiar guises or masquerading as something quite different.

The most perfect disguises were worn by the streamlined locomotives of the inter-war period. Who, for instance, would have guessed that an orthodox-shape 'Sandringham' 4–6–0 lay beneath the sleek cowl that covered Nos 2859 and 2870, the engines which regularly worked the 'East Anglian'? Certainly there must have been many who were surprised when the familiar form of a 'Duchess' emerged from the smooth cocoon which, until after the war, encased Stanier's 'Coronation' Pacifics. The streamlining served a practical purpose but it had, perhaps, even more value as a fancy dress intended to catch the eye of the public and create an 'image' of speed and modernity.

The same cannot be said of Bulleid's Pacifics. The air-smoothed outer casing was intended to facilitate cleaning, but unfortunately it also rendered many parts somewhat inaccessible. From 1956, British Railways stripped it off all the Merchant Navy Pacifics and over half the lightweights, preferring ease of maintenance to cleanliness and simplicity of outline.

At the same time the chain-driven valve gear was removed from the obscurity of its oil bath between the frames and orthodox Walschaerts valve gear was fitted outside the driving wheels. These changes unmasked a striking machine but many admirers of Bulleid's masterpiece missed the homogeneity and clean lines of the original.

Apart from the Pacifics, Bulleid also designed the notorious Q1 class 'Austerity' 0–6–0's. No one has ever been tempted to describe the external treatment of these locomotives as fancy dress. Yet it was an appropriate attire for the war years and is interesting in that it completely disguised the fact that these engines were, in several respects, a development of Maunsell's Q class locomotives. And, whatever may be said about their external appearance, it is impossible to obscure the fact that they did yeoman service for the Southern Railway and, later, the Southern Region.

The Great Western Railway tried to jump on the bandwagon when the vogue for

Collett's answer to the streamliners – an orthodox King class 4—6—0 No 6014 *King Henry VII* fitted with domed smokebox door covering, fairings around the cylinders, chimney and safety valve bonnet, and a wedge-shaped front to the cab. A Castle class locomotive was similarly clothed, but otherwise the experiment was not repeated.

Lurking beneath the 'Mini-A4' streamlining seen in this view of No 2859 *East Anglian* (*above*) was a perfectly orthodox Gresley class B17 4—6—0. Sister locomotive No 2870 *City of London* was similarly cocooned in 1937, and the pair thereafter regularly worked the 'East Anglian' express from Liverpool Street. In 1951, the streamlined casing was removed from both locomotives and B1-type boilers were fitted. It is in this final condition that No 61670 *City of London* is seen (*below*) passing East London Junction on June 14, 1958, with a Yarmouth South Town-Liverpool Street train.

[*R. E. Vincent*

In their heyday, Stanier's streamlined Coronation Pacifics sported speed lines which, on some 'Royal Scot' stock, was continued along the length of the train. In this view, however (*above*), more orthodox stock is in use as No 6227 *Duchess of Devonshire* comes off Hest Bank Troughs with the up 'Royal Scot'. [*W. Hubert Foster*

When, in 1946, work began on the removal of the streamlined casing from the Coronation Pacifics, many were surprised to see that beneath the smooth casing was an orthodox Duchess class Pacific. Only the cut-away footplate ahead of the cylinders and the slightly depressed top of the smokebox front reveal the origin of *Duchess of Devonshire* in this shot (*below*) after rebuilding, again in charge of the up 'Royal Scot', but this time passing Upperby Shed. Later, the depressed top of the smokebox front was modified to standard 'Duchess' shape. [*Eric Treacy*

At the same time that the Coronations were being de-streamlined, the Bulleid air-smoothed Merchant Navy and West Country Pacifics were still being built. Many variations in the design of the casing were tried before the final form, seen on No 35027 *Port Line* (*above*) was evolved. Earlier engines were modified to much the same style, but still some difficulties persisted.

It was not surprising, therefore, that ten years later, in 1956, work began on the rebuilding of the Bulleid Pacifics. The air-smoothed casing was removed, and the efficient but inaccessible Bulleid valve gear was replaced with orthodox Walschaerts gear. Thus modified, *Port Line* sets out from Bournemouth West (*below*) for Waterloo with the up 'Bournemouth Belle' on June 14, 1965.

[*Derek Cross*

streamlining was at its height and endeavoured to give a modish look to a 'King' and a 'Castle'. To many this attempt by the GWR to 'get with it' looked about as appropriate as a mini skirt worn by a dowager. It was, of course, little more than a fancy dress and scarcely disguised the identity of the locomotive wearing it. For that reason it was approved by the distinguished industrial designer Raymond Loewy, who was himself responsible for the external fashioning of the Pennsylvania Railroad's streamlined locomotives. He maintained that a steam locomotive should always look like a steam locomotive and that streamlining should not be allowed to obscure the essential character of the engine – an opinion that should carry some weight and may cause some critics to revise their views on Collett's controversial essay in the prevailing idiom.

From the Great Western 'Castle' let us turn to some earlier locomotives bearing the same generic name – the 'Castles' of the Highland Railway. The drawings for these locomotives – a passenger version of the famous 'Big Goods' – were in course of preparation when David Jones, the locomotive superintendent of the Highland Railway, met his death. They were completed by his successor, Peter Drummond. No doubt, had Jones finished the work himself, the new design would have been practically identical with his earlier goods engine, except for the somewhat larger driving wheels. But Peter Drummond had his own very different ideas on how an engine should look and disguised the similarity between the new locomotive and his predecessor's design by dressing it up in his brother's clothes. He used Dugald Drummond's pattern of cab and boiler mountings and even went so far as to provide the 'Castles' with eight wheeled 'Water Carts' like the ones his brother harnessed to the 'Iron Horses' of the South Western Railway! Only the close spacing of the driving wheels revealed the basic affinity between the Jones Goods and the 'Castles'.

It must be admitted that the 'styling' of the 'Castles' was much more accomplished than that of the 'Big Goods'. The distinctly odd louvred chimney was replaced by one of shapely pattern, very similar again to those devised by Dugald Drummond, and the large ugly sand boxes which disfigured the leading splashers of Jones' 4–6–0 were cleverly hidden within the combined splasher covering the leading pairs of driving wheels. The rear splashers, instead of being arbitrarily chopped in half by the cab, were merged with it to form a single unit, and at the front end, graceful curves took the place of straight lines where the main frames rose above the platform to support the smokebox.

Other features peculiar to the Drummond engines were the marine-type big ends and the steam reversing gear which did away with the

Highland Railway 'Jones Goods' 4—6—0 No 103 after restoration to working order and original livery by the Scottish Region in 1959.

[*British Railways*

When Peter Drummond came to the Highland Railway, a passenger version of the 'Jones Goods' was being prepared. He continued the work, but incorporated his own design of chimney and cab. He also fitted the sandboxes between the front and centre splashers, and merged the rear splasher with the side-sheets of the cab, as seen here, on No 140 *Taymouth Castle.*

necessity for a large reversing rod and contributed to their exceptionally neat appearance. The 'Castles' were as successful as they were handsome, and certainly worthy successors to the 'Big Goods'. For this David Jones deserves the credit because, despite the virtually complete disguise, the design was basically his.

Midland pride was ever loath to admit that any good thing ever came out of Crewe (and vice versa). So it was only to be expected that Sir Henry Fowler would disguise the North Western origin of his design for the 7F 0–8–0s (or G3s, as they were sometimes known) which he built for the LMS. The G2s of the LNWR formed the basis of the new design, but externally the disguise was perfect – Midland in every detail including cab, tender, firebox, dome, smokebox and chimney.

It would be convenient for present purposes to be able to cite Fowler's 'Patriots' as a further example of a North Western design in Midland guise but this would hardly be true. For the 'Patriots', although officially described as rebuilt 'Claughtons', were virtually new engines; the whole conception of the design was radically altered both inside and out. Only the wheel centres from two of the original engines remained.

The Midland Railway did, however, make every attempt to disguise the origins of the LTSR engines which they took over. Not only the red livery but also the Derby pattern of chimney and smokebox door effectively changed the character of these fine machines and gave them a strong Midland flavour.

Johnson and Deeley also succeeded in giving a thoroughly Midland look to a type conceived by a North Eastern engineer. Walter Smith had successfully applied his system of compounding to T. W. Worsdell's NER 4–4–0 No 1619. It had one high pressure and two low pressure cylinders. His friend Johnson was greatly impressed with the idea and built his own version of it – the first of the famous Midland compounds – and decked it out in his sumptuous crimson livery. There were independent valve gears for the high and low pressure cylinders and a changeover valve which admitted live steam to the low pressure cylinders for extra power on heavy gradients. Considerable skill was required of the driver in manipulating all these controls to advantage. It remained for Deeley to rationalize and simplify arrange-

As a basic heavy goods engine, the ex-LNWR G1 and G2 class 0—8—0s gave sterling service well into BR days. Several were rebuilt by the LMS with Belpaire boilers, including No 9190, here seen at the head of an up freight near Strines on the Great Central and Midland Joint Line.

[R. D. Pollard

ments. At the same time he transformed the appearance of the engines into their final well-known form. Nevertheless, despite the varied guises, the basic conception remained unchanged.

Johnson himself had seen one of his own designs transplanted and taking root, if not exactly flourishing, when his assistant, Robert Billinton, left Derby to superintend the locomotive department at Brighton, where he built a supremely elegant 4–4–0 of the Johnson type. Its provenance was partially disguised by the yellow livery, raised platform and the use of Stroudley's dome and a modified form of his cab. But the general proportions of the locomotive gave the game away, and there was no disguising the Midland derivation of the chimney and the typically slender boiler with its attractively waisted smokebox.

The graceful reverse curves of the platform characterised succeeding Brighton express engines including that most majestic of all tank engines, L. B. Billinton's 'Remembrance'.

After the electrification of the Brighton and Eastbourne lines the Southern Railway had little use for very large express tank engines, so 'Remembrance' and her sisters were divested of the chaste covering provided by the long

After Grouping, Fowler produced his own design of 0—8—0, based on the LNWR engines, but sporting typically Midland cab, chimney and smokebox. Here is No 49667 in early BR days.

[R. K. Evans

In April, 1914, the first of L. B. Billinton's graceful L class 4—6—4T locomotives, No 327, was turned out of Brighton Works. No 328 soon followed, but wartime conditions prevented further construction, and it was 1922 before the last of the class, No 333, appeared. It was named *Remembrance* in memory of the employees of the LBSCR who gave their lives in the Great War, and is seen here in early Southern Railway days.

When the Southern electrified the Brighton, Worthing and Eastbourne lines between 1933 and 1935, the LBSCR L class became redundant. Maunsell therefore rebuilt them as 4—6—0 tender engines, gave them large bogie tenders, reclassified them N15X and put them to work on the Western Section, where we see No 2328 *Hackworth* at the head of a down Salisbury train near Winchfield in 1947. [*M. W. Earley*

side tanks and were converted into tender engines. Maunsell did his best, it would appear, to disguise the Brighton origin of the engines. He applied his own style of cab and chimney, attached to them some ex-LSWR tenders and, in belated regard for their outraged modesty, fitted blinkers to mask their identity. But it seems that nothing could atone for the violence done to them, for it is said that they refused to render such good service afterwards. Perhaps the reduction in adhesive weight on the driving wheels when the tanks were removed was partly responsible.

Maunsell's 'Rivers', which had proved unstable under certain running conditions, had earlier been similarly converted from tank into tender engines, but the reverse procedure was more common elsewhere. Barton-Wright's 'Ironclads' of the LYR were turned into saddle-tank engines by Aspinall, while many well-known types appeared in both guises, as tender engines and as tank engines. Among these were Churchward's 'Counties' and the North Western 'Precursors', 'Princes' and 0–8–0s – these last forming the basis of Beame's mighty 0–8–4 tank engines. A more modern example, the 9400 class engines of the Great Western, on close inspection revealed themselves to be none other than Collett 2251 class 0–6–0s laden with panniers and propelled by smaller wheels. But surely the grandest of all such adaptations

Introduced in 1947, the Hawksworth 9400 class 0—6—0PT, of which 9405 (*above*) was a member, was in many ways a tank version, with smaller wheels, of the Collett 2251 class 0—6—0 tender locomotives introduced in 1930. An example of the latter, No 3215, is seen (*below*) on the Somerset and Dorset at Templecombe with a train from Highbridge on June 28, 1962. It is signalled onto the spur leading up to Templecombe Junction Station on the South Western main line. [*A. Swain, Derek Cross*

was Hughes' magnificent four cylinder 'Baltic' tank engine, a tank version of his massive 'Dreadnought' 4–6–0 express passenger tender engine.

D. E. Marsh could do little to disguise the Great Northern derivation of the 'Atlantics' he built for the LBSCR when he relinquished his post of chief assistant to H. A. Ivatt and accepted the locomotive superintendency of the 'Brighton'. The Great Northern and Brighton Atlantics were almost identical in form, the southern version being more sophisticated in its external 'styling'. Moreover, the umber livery in which Marsh's locomotives were dressed was actually much less 'fancy' than the bright apple green of their Great Northern sisters, but it was smart and serviceable. At the amalgamation they changed liveries again but they could not compare with Dugald Drummond's 4–4–0s for the sheer variety of the colourful guises in which they appeared.

When Drummond designed his epoch-making 'Abbotsford' for the North British Railway he might have labelled it 'also available in full range of attractive colours'. He himself built similar 4–4–0s for other companies, painting them blue for the Caledonian and light green for the South Western (altering the chimney a little at the same time), while his brother Peter built some for the Highland (the 'Small Bens'), decking them out in the darker green livery of that company. With the formation of the LMS at grouping in 1923, the Caledonian and Highland engines entered yet another area of the spectrum – red. Remembering the drabness that was to follow, it is cheering to recollect such resplendent guises. They provide a happy note on which to conclude this exercise in detection.

Before D. Earle Marsh joined the LBSCR in 1905, he had been working under Ivatt on the Great Northern, so it is hardly surprising that one of his first designs was for an Atlantic very akin to those produced for the GNR by his old master. There were certain detail improvements on Marsh's engines, such as tidier cylinders and a slightly more civilised cab, but nevertheless the similarity between Marsh's LBSCR No 37 of 1905 (*left*) and Ivatt's GNR No 1460 of 1902 (*below*) is most striking.

Parcels and Milk

The evening sun casts long shadows across the platform at Queens Road, Battersea as S15 class 4—6—0 No 30842 rattles by on the down South Western main line with the 7.02pm parcels train for the Bournemouth line on July 27, 1964.

[Brian Stephenson

Double-chimneyed Castle class 4—6—0 No 5057 *Earl Waldegrave* restarts the 3.00pm milk empties from West Ealing away from a signal check at Iver on September 14, 1963.

[*M. Pope*

Warship class diesel hydraulic No D824 *Highflyer* hurries through Seaton Junction with the 11.30am Brighton-Plymouth train on August 8, 1964, while in the background West Country class Pacific No 34015 *Exmouth* shunts milk wagons to the adjacent dairy.

[*W. L. Underhay*

Castle class 4—6—0 No 7025 *Sudeley Castle* crosses to the down main line at West Ealing and sets out for the West Country with a train of returning empty milk tanks.

[*R. C. Riley*

Also beginning its return journey to the West Country is this train of empty milk tanks from Morden, seen here on the first stage of its journey, coming off the Sutton line at Wimbledon on May 29, 1965, in the charge of grimy BR standard class 5 4—6—0 No 73086 *The Green Knight.*

[*R. A. Panting*

Hard Class to Vladivostok

C. PORTWAY

Engraved upon the heart of every Englishman there is a railway train. The etching may have worn a little thin with the passage of our adult years and the frustrations of commuting on packed, late and strike-bound suburban services, but it still may be discerned. Our dormant love of trains stands second only to that of animals. Way down the list among the 'also rans' come our wives, our children and our cars, and these not necessarily in that order!

Even so, nine days on the Trans-Siberian Express is not everybody's cup of tea. For me it was a boyhood dream, the ultimate of railway journeys. Like most dreams, its accomplishment had to be pushed a little and paid for not only in cash but in kind. My family's holiday went to the altar of sacrifice, my wife – like all wives – seeing little amusement in being rattled across the world by train. Mine, in particular, had no desire to go to Russia either. She's Czech.

Let me say here and now that the Trans-Siberian Express is the best thing in Russia. Some of us in our enthusiastic innocence have vague notions of the Trans-Siberian as an old Klondyke cow-catcher locomotive pulling a line of open-end Czarist wagons across eternal snow. In fact it is probably one of the most comfortable trains in both Europe and Asia. The wider Russian gauge ensures spaciousness, the coaches are kept spotlessly clean and its time-table is strictly adhered to. Best of all, it is the one place in the whole of the Soviet Union in which you can live with its citizens.

There are actually three trains that cover all or part of the 5,778 mile line. There is the 'Russia' hauling a train between Moscow and Vladivostok daily in the summer and four times weekly in winter, there is the 'Baikal' to Irkutsk, chief town of Siberia, twice and four times weekly, and the 'Yenisei' running daily to Krasnoyarsk. Vladivostok however is the end of the line and the logical terminus of the Trans-Siberian so, from the start, my shirt was on the 'Russia' or, in the unromantic parlance of Soviet Railways, Train No 2.

There was a snag however. Vladivostok is off the tourist beat. And in Russia this means 'Out of bounds'. It is a top naval base and is on the Chinese border. It is definitely a place where nosey tourists are not welcome. There are in fact only three places along the route of the Trans-Siberian Railway that they are. These are Novosibirsk, Irkutsk and Khabarovsk, the last 500 miles north of Vladivostok. A fourth place, the small port of Nakhodka, only thirty miles short, can be visited in transit if you are going to Japan. Omsk, with its neighbour, Tomsk, are 'off limits' too. But it was Vladivostok upon which I had set my sights.

For me the journey had started at the Hook of Holland in a Soviet through coach on the Ost-West Express. Two Germanies and two Berlins, each competing for bigger and better border controls, at least prepared me for the savage procedures at the Russian frontier. They do not put down the welcome mat at Brest or any other of the official crossing points either. Moscow is usually the second introduction to the Soviet Union and first impressions – particularly those of its hotels – are so awful that to climb aboard another train is a pleasure.

The organisation that controls your every move in Russia is Intourist. At surveillance it is first class. At looking after the requirements of tourists, of satisfying their whims and wishes, it is a dead loss. They prefer their tourists in squads, of course. I was a loner and one of the awkward brigade. In all towns and cities open to tourists they have their minions. They meet your train or your aeroplane and hunt you down however crowded the station or airport. To be fair, these minions are usually nice people working for an impossible organisation riddled with unbelievable bureaucracy. Its hotels vary. They feed you and lend you a bed to sleep on, but to obtain even these you need the patience of Job, a warped sense of humour and about a fiver per night. Nothing goes right; things seldom work except the telephones, which are loud in their insistence on early calls you've not ordered.

To crown everything I had a problem. Because my agent in London had not done his homework correctly, the Soviet Embassy had seen fit to issue me with only a temporary visa – one just for Moscow of 7 days' validity. In the Russian capital I was supposed to have it replaced with a more comprehensive document. But the Embassy had reckoned without Intourist and its blind insistence to adhesion to the programme. And my programme did not allow for detours to ministries for the purpose of rectifying lame visas. My bleats remained unheard.

Moscow no doubt grows on you. I just had time for a stroll in Red Square, a glimpse of the dead Lenin, an inspection of the statue-laden underground and a visit to GUM and the Bolshoi between endless reception formalities at the Bucharest Hotel and my reporting to the Jaroslav Station next day. Jaroslav Station was even more of a madhouse than the Bucharest Hotel. Its platforms had become separated from the station and it was bulging at the seams with what I can only describe as nomads. Few people seemed to be travelling. Most were living there. Nowhere could I find any reference to the great Trans-Siberian Express, or even a train No 2. There were no officials to ask, so I went to a ticket window, put on a 'little boy lost' face and pointed to my travel voucher. Whatever impression the border people might give, a Russian will do anything to help you. This one slammed down his shutter in the face of the person at the head of the queue, led me to my train and saw me off.

The Trans-Siberian is a window on Russia and the Russians. One can look out to see Russia and look in to see Russians. Both are fascinating. The supporting feature does not become immediately apparent. Word has to circulate that there is an Englishman on the train. In the meantime there is Russia.

The first excitement was Zagorosk, the former Sergievo and the Canterbury of Russia, with the turnip domes of its great monastery flashing gold in the sun. Jaroslav revealed the Volga, provoking adoration all around, but here it was no more than a wide muddy stream washing the backsides of factories. Kirov was but a noise in the night. A river called Chusovaya acted as the western border of both Siberia and Asia and Sverdlovsk was a great hulk of a town with chimneys, like pencils, scrawling rude words on the sky. Somewhere between Sverdlovsk and Perm had been a few gentle downs and I wondered where I had got the idea that the Urals were mountains.

You cannot but help pondering upon the conception and history of this astounding line as train after train crashes by in the opposite direction, at intervals of very few minutes, full of the sinews of life – and death, for many carry the tools of war. Czar Alexander III started it in 1890. Cost was no object, for its prime purpose was military. Sections of it blossomed and were put to use haphazardly. Haphazard, too, were the laying methods, much track having to be replaced in later years. In 1895 the line reached Irkutsk, capital of Siberia, but the great mass of Lake Baikal baulked further progress. In 1898 the rails from east and west met near Chita, the link across Baikal being maintained by a Newcastle-built ferry in Summer and by a temporary track laid directly across the ice in Winter. The dangerous Winter schedules were finally safeguarded when a line was hacked through the granite mountains around the southern shore. Luxury expresses never envisaged before (or since!) went into regular service in 1903, in stark contrast to the trains of *teplushki* wagons carrying convicts to servitude. The wars of 1904 and 1914–18 suspended the luxury traffic, and during the latter the Trans-Siberian fell into the hands of both Red and White armies, as well as Semeonov's bandits, who used trains against one another almost as jousting knights of earlier conflicts. Communism brought mis-

The ornate columns and lighting of the Yaroslavsky Station, Moscow, contrast strongly with the bulky, modern lines of the ten-car ER1-type electric multiple unit waiting to depart. [*J. N. Westwood*

eries greater than those of war, and when Stalin died some 15 million souls rotted in camps in Siberia and beyond. Maybe they could find a spark of comfort from the railway. Their predecessors had to walk those 5000 terrible miles.

Now, life on the Trans-Siberian is refreshingly aimless. You wake up in the morning, your watch tells you it is 8 o'clock, but you know it does not matter a hoot since, moving east, it will alter anyway and not just with the passage of time. Your berth is comfortable. There is no need to get up and no incentive or reason for doing so. You have little to look forward to and nothing to avoid. You lie on your seat, justifiably inert, seeing all there is to see without the slightest effort. Mostly there is nothing to look at, but there is no reason to stop looking. The one chore is making up your own bed. And this only because the girl coach attendant is so busy polishing the brasswork and vacuum-cleaning the carpets she has simply no time. Nobody is allowed off the train until she has rubbed down the handrails and doorknobs. The lavatories right along the train are a treat and nobody pinches the soap or the paper.

As a break from monotony there is the restaurant car, full of noise and movement. The food is wholesome if not of the variety indicated by the vast menu. Obtaining a meal takes time anywhere in the Soviet Union, but on the Trans-Siberian you have that commodity. Some western travellers in Russia purchase food coupons from Intourist prior to their journey. This is a mistake, for even should you be able to stow away all the food to which you will be entitled, you would pay more for it. In fact the cost of a soft class ticket from Moscow right across to Khabarovsk need only be £36, with adequate eating at less than £1 a day making it not only the longest but also one of the cheapest train journies in the world. Caviar is available from the restaurant car immediately following periodic stores replenishment, but it doesn't last long.

Whether you want a meal or just a beer, a visit to the restaurant car is a social event. It is also the spawning ground for the invitations that start coming in on the second day. Sometimes, after stretching your legs along the tracks at a wayside station, a Russian will be standing awkwardly by your soft-class compartment door. The rigmarole of conversation in two utterly opposed tongues commences until a few common basics make it understood that your presence is required in Compartment 14, Coach No 8. You go to Compartment 14, Coach No 8 and are vigorously entertained, often wined and dined and asked a multitude of questions on every conceivable subject. There is always someone who speaks a little English or German or French. Then the chain reaction begins and one of the hosts will issue a subsequent invitation. One, I remember, was for breakfast from a Red Army colonel. A true Red Army breakfast he had promised, and I looked forward to the equivalent of our bacon and eggs. But it had consisted of a tea tumbler of vodka, alone, unsupported and raw. Occasionally an exchange in the restaurant car would snowball into a general discussion, one of which ended in my lecturing all and sundry on Vietnam! It had been that evening that I had met Peter.

In London I had tried to get permission to visit Vladivostok. In Moscow I had tried to get permission to visit Vladivostok. I was to try again in Novosibirsk, in Irkutsk and in Khabarovsk. But everybody made it very plain that I could not visit Vladivostok. Nobody would give me any reasons beyond the unsatisfactory half-explanation that there were no Intourist facilities and that it was a naval base. Had they not been so adamant about my not going I might not have bothered. And then Peter, Peter the student from Komsomolsk, full of home-made brandy and a sucker for my English cigarettes, said he would get me a ticket for Vladivostok.

I stopped off at Novosibirsk and inspected Academgorodok, the city of scientific establishments that Intourist fondly imagined to be a tourist attraction. I stopped off at the older Irkutsk to paddle, with a clutch of East German holidaymakers, in the nippy waters of the giant Lake Baikal. And I stopped off at Khabarovsk for the simple reason that tourists not bound for Japan can go no farther. What other reasons there are evade me unless it be the enormous Amur River. Four days they had given me in Khabarovsk when I had only asked for two.

My estimation of Russian towns, it might be noticed, does not rise very high. Nor could I get much change out of their residents. Talking to strangers on a train provides no problems, but once in a town you are shunned like the plague. This does not add to the qualities of cities that have little enough to offer in the first place. The spirit may be strong but the flesh is weak. Only in the anonymity of the train do Russians emerge from their shells.

The best season for Siberia is Autumn. It is a world of trees – pine, cedar, larch and birch. They call it the *taiga*. It goes unbroken for hundreds, indeed thousands, of miles. In the north, in the permafrost, a larch takes a century to grow. In the south are tiger-infested jungles. In between one could fit the United States with plenty of room to spare. The sun shining on the Autumn colouring of the trees turns Siberia into a gigantic vat of burnished gold. Occasionally the sea of trees breaks into a storm of rock, as at Baikal and beyond Chita. The mountains of Mongolia and Manchuria show blue in the distance. Tiny churchless villages of square wooden houses – *izbas* – huddle together in a clearing, fighting a battle for existence against the remorseless *taiga*. Their loneliness has you by the throat. Perhaps this is why Russians talk on trains.

Peter had guts enough to talk to me in a town. To my surprise, he kept the appointment we made on the train and, somewhat overawed by his own boldness, came to see me at my Khabarovsk hotel. Together we took a tram to the station. He left me outside while the deed was done and came out wielding both ticket and hard-class berth reservation. I paid him the amount owing, as well as a packet of cigarettes for his trouble, and invited him to spend the remainder of the afternoon with me. But the enormity of his crime had sapped his strength. He shook my hand with an embarrassed smile and withdrew.

Examination of the ticket revealed that it was valid only for a single journey to Vladivostok. This would mean applying for a return berth reservation – compulsory on long-distance journies in the USSR – in Vladivostok, an action which filled me with a certain amount of foreboding. The less people who knew that I was in forbidden territory the better.

In the light of the *fait accompli* of the ticket, I made my plans. I had four days at Khabarovsk and one had already expired. I had time to reach Vladivostok, spend eight hours in that city and return to Khabarovsk before my scheduled departure on the fourth day. Both the outward and return journies would be made overnight and I'd still be back for my last night in Khabarovsk. If all went well nobody would know that I had been away.

The train was again the 'Russia', the same east-bound Trans-Siberian Express as had brought me to Khabarovsk 24 hours earlier. I left my luggage in my bedroom, slunk out of the hotel at midnight and arrived at the station to see the great express slide into its alloted platform in a sweat of steam.

I found my more humble hard class coach at the rear without difficulty. The girl attendant gave me an odd glance and twice checked my ticket. I thought she was going to start asking questions, but a scuffle at the other end of her domain sent her scurrying off. With more difficulty I located my berth amongst the prostrate, snoring, smelly humanity. An old woman was sleeping loudly on the berth whose number corresponded with that on my ticket but the one above was free. I clambered up amidst a chorus of grunts. As soon as the train moved the attendant appeared with my bedding which I spread awkwardly. I didn't bother to undress.

On the whole it was not a bad night. The class of travel refers to the bunks. 'Soft' indicates four sprung bunks in a closed compartment. 'Hard' describes a more crowded wooden bunk-filled open coach. But since bedding is issued to both classes of passenger the texture of the bunks themselves is immaterial. The 'Hards' are very much more communal which can be both advantageous or disadvantageous depending upon individual outlook.

From my vantage point on the top bunk I watched the coach come alive in the morning. Children's voices, in laughter and complaint, rose in volume as parental control laxed and big women contorted themselves replacing or tightening garments removed or loosened in the night.

I lay contentedly dozing and reading until quite late. My bunk was too high for me to see out of the window and I did not want to draw attention to myself until it was necessary. The train did not reach Vladivostok until one in the afternoon so I had the whole morning to lie low. Then the coach attendant began collecting bedding and I was forced to emerge.

There was a flurry of excitement as it flashed through the community that an Englishman had joined it. There was amazement, too, for tourists never travelled hard class. I tried to tell a hushed audience that this was no fault of the tourists and that their own organisation – Intourist – was to blame! I hope they got the message, for the compulsory segregation in hotels and elsewhere was a source of great bitterness among simpler Russians.

I was invited to share breakfast with the owners of the bunks around me and soon was replete with salami, hard boiled egg, fish and cheese. I was fussed over by old men and women of peasant stock whose gnarled hands kept passing me more food every time my own were empty. A refusal did no good, only provoking noisy indignation. Tea from the samovar washed the whole lot down and I then had to play a question and answer game on the subject of personal possessions – always a sure bet for conversation in the Soviet Union, where ownership of a car puts you in the millionaire class.

Outside the grey morning was increasing the sombreness of steeply rolling countryside that reminded me of the lowlands of Scotland. Uncultivated grasslands rising above the undulations were, in turn, overlooked by hills and a narrow road ran for miles alongside the railway. Later the hills became slag heaps, universally ugly, and some birch woods offered the illusion that we were back in Europe. Yet China was but five miles distant across that dew-laden grass.

We stopped at Nadejdinskaya, the junction for Nakhodka, and among my fellow-passengers strolling on the platform – many flaunting jazzy pyjama suits – I noticed that police were more in evidence than usual. They were infesting the train, too, and my bunk really did live up to its class as I retired, subdued, to its bare unhospitable refuge.

The few minutes it had fallen behind schedule the train made up in the last thirty miles and we drew into Vladivostok station exactly on time. I felt a glow of satisfaction. With the last 500 miles from Khabarovsk I had, whatever happened next, accomplished my goal. I was nearly six thousand miles east of Moscow, nearly eight thousand from home. I had reached the Pacific on the other side of the World and, except for the English Channel – not much larger than some of the Siberian rivers – it had all been done by trains.

Vladivostok means 'ruler of the East'. Count Muraviev, who had a hand in the colonising of Khabarovsk, selected the site for the port after the treaty of Aigun in 1858 by which the district was ceded to Russia. In 1860 the first settlers arrived and the port itself came into being twelve years later – to the discomfort of Japan, who had no great desire to have a Russian naval base on her doorstep. But Vladivostok is not only a naval port. Its four-by-one-mile harbour, kept ice-free all the year round, is home to the Soviet whaling flotillas and her Far Eastern fishing fleet. The town itself is heavily industrialised.

It is overpopulated with soldiers as well as sailors. I found this out before I had left its rambling station as a battalion of fully-armed troops disgorged from a train onto the same platform as ourselves. I went in search of the ticket office. If reservations had to be made, I thought it wise to get my oar in early. I possessed a piece of paper containing the Russian for 'A return hard class ticket to

A rare opportunity to make direct comparisons between British and Russian loading gauges was afforded at this exhibition at Munich. Being shunted into position are, on the left, a new couchette car for the Trans-Siberian Railway coupled, on the right, to a then-new BR Mk II corridor first.

Khabarovsk, please', so I pushed it at the face behind the grill. The face spoke words to the effect that I must obtain reservations from an office in the town and pushed my paper back with an address scribbled on it.

The town I discovered to be exceedingly awful. Even Novosibirsk was fairyland in comparison. Ports anywhere can rarely boast of exotic surroundings but those of Vladivostok, even with its backdrop of hills rising behind, were truly functional. I found the office with the help of a middle-aged citizen muffled up as if it were already midwinter. He walked with me a considerable distance out of his way and refused my thank-you offering of a cigarette.

The office seemed to be a department of the railway. It was pillared, high-ceilinged and full of travel posters – mostly of places unattainable to Russians! No one spoke English. I didn't think they would. My request for a reservation was understood but something seemed to be required to support the application. It was not a passport and anyway I had no intention of giving mine up unless strictly necessary, since the visa was now ten days out of date and I was six thousand miles off course. It could only confuse the issue. They kept invoking the name of Intourist, which didn't help any, for they knew, as I knew, that there was no Intourist office in Vladivostok. Then I had a brainwave and mumbled the word 'diplomat', not quite certain if I wasn't making things worse. From my wallet I withdrew and displayed my driving licence, regimental association membership card and Barclaycard. Each came under interested scrutiny, the Barclaycard scoring highest points. Shrugs followed, but they were constructive shrugs – the kind that says 'What the hell, anyway'. Came the capitulation and the indication that I was to return for both ticket and reservation that evening. Thankfully I fled.

I have never been able to hide a guilty conscience, and the one I bore as I skulked down those depressing Vladivostok streets was the most monumental ever. The fact annoyed me, for I could not accept that I was doing wrong. 'Don't go and do anything silly,' had been the refrain from my loved ones as I left home and here I was flouting the rules simply to satisfy a whim. In my heart I knew the source of the conscience.

Certain elementary precautions had been taken. My camera, for instance, remained in my Khabarovsk hotel. I looked reasonably non-descript Russian in a pair of thick fawn slacks and leather jacket. I had not shaved that morning. But I still jumped at the sight of the expressionless little man standing in what was almost certainly Karl Marx Square. I had long realized the significance of the Lenin-style cloth cap and ill-fitting overcoat. Years before I had cut my teeth in the secret police recognition game, both Nazi and Communist, and this specimen was no different. I sheered away but when I stopped to tie a shoe-lace he wasn't following. Later, I thought one was and led an imaginary watchdog a circuitous route through a department store. But I suspect that the only person I was tiring was myself.

Suddenly I saw the sea. It was brown and lifeless, but the moment notched a milestone in my life. I have seen the Pacific before off California. I've even swum in it among surroundings far pleasanter. But that glimpse between an unfinished building block and a sheaf of dockside cranes will shine the brighter in my memory.

To approach the sea I had to walk along the harbour front. Shipping of every description jostled the docks, which hummed with activity. I watched deck-swabbing on trawlers and whalers, and the unloading of crates from cargo vessels. All the while, in the background, the gaunt forms of cruisers and destroyers showed stark against the sky. Seamen and sailors, all speaking the language of the sea in spite of their contrasting dress, thronged the dockside. Soldiers, out of place in maritime territory, self-consciously lounged around a convoy of heavy lorries and I felt their eyes following me as I walked stiffly by. Red slogans announced: LENIN – OUR TEACHER AND OUR FRIEND from wooden hoardings. They alone shattered the illusion that this port could be anywhere in the world.

I had a meal in a stand-up buffet serving frankfurter-type sausage, cabbage and potato. It was a rough dock-area kind of place but its exclusive supply of sausage and mash offered a minimum of chat. Late in the afternoon I walked around the corner of a back street into a funeral cortège. The double row of deliberate men in white shirts escorted an open coffin carried shoulder high. Behind them followed a gaggle of women with no apparent sense of the dignity of the occasion.

Some of those back streets housed families living in poverty pure and simple. There is no other word for it. Many left wing writers on Russia do not recognize that poverty can exist in a communist state and it gives me no pleasure to prove them wrong. Perhaps this is the reason for the exclusion of tourists from Vladivostok.

With dusk I entered a bookshop to browse around the shelves, as I invariably do when at a loose end. Most of the literature was political and deadly dull. Collet's in Holborn could put on a better show. A man recognized me as English (so much for my efforts to look otherwise!) and behind the pages of a large volume he told me something of his years in both Hitler and Stalin camps and my heart went out to him. Now he was a man without rights and without hope.

I left to return to the railway office and then to the station. I'd seen enough of Vladivostok. On the way I passed a cripple, horribly disfigured. On the man's jacket was a treble row of medal ribbons and I realized that he was one of the legion of maimed ex-servicemen who had fought for a country that now exiled its broken ranks to places not visited by foreign tourists. To me this was perhaps the ugliest facet of the Soviet Union; one that never reaches the pages of the glib Intourist handouts.

The collection of my ticket produced no incidents and I offered no arguments even when I noticed it was for soft class travel. I still had two hours to wait before departure of the train but in the station I felt on safer ground. Hadn't I made a simple mistake and come to Vladivostok instead of Nakhodka and was now waiting like a good citizen for the return train? A bit thin perhaps but it sounded better here in the station than it would have done in the vicinity of those battleships.

I immersed myself in my book propped up against a pillar and was thus engaged when I felt someone staring at me. I changed position and caught sight of my watcher. He was another member of the Lenin cloth cap brigade. Forcing myself to read a couple more paragraphs I stood my ground, then, as if tiring of the book, closed it and ambled off towards the platforms. A convenient lavatory, masked by the left-luggage room, offered sanctuary and in I went – straight into a vast woman, arms akimbo. I had a split second to choose between the female mammoth and the secret policeman. I chose the policeman, executed a smart right about turn, and emerged discomforted from the ladies toilet. But the sleuth was not in sight, having either failed to follow me or, as I intended, passed by. Tiring of cops and robbers, I took refuge in the pungent tobacco fog of a waiting hall.

My soft empty compartment was a treat. The coach girl gave me bedding and a long, hard but not unfriendly look to go with it. I thought ruefully of my ten pounds of bed that had gone for a burton in my Khabarovsk hotel. But my dismal little excursion had not been wasted. Maybe it had been even cheap at the price.

Back at Khabarovsk, Intourist gave me what could almost be described as a royal welcome. I was obviously the first tourist they had 'lost' and the return of the prodigal son had them rushing over to my hotel full of the joys of spring. I could tell that the carefully guarded questions were not simply a personal interest in where I had been. The hotel had reported my absence, I was told, and all the staff of the Intourist office had been *most* concerned. What *had* I been doing? They were in an unfortunate position. To have demanded an explanation would have put Intourist in a wrong light. And as I wasn't telling they could only jump to conclusions. My answers were evasive in the extreme, giving the impression possibly of shame, so they jumped to the wrong conclusion. Firmly convinced that I had spent a couple of nights with a girl, they next wanted to know who. I made no denials and as their concern was obviously centred upon some female 'deviationist' whose political thoughts I may have corrupted, more than my own morals, I let them stew. Finally, I got a mild lecture on inconsiderateness.

The rest of the day I spent behaving myself in Khabarovsk. Next day I flew west. I hadn't asked to fly but Intourist had designated it and that was that. Back at Novosibirsk we changed direction and flew South across the barren corrugations of the Kirgiz Steppe to Alma Ata – 'City of Apples' – grovelling at the foot of the Tien Shan – 'Mountains of Heaven' – and onto Tashkent; a new Tashkent of modern concrete. There is a perfectly adequate railway covering the southward route but its trains – if there are any – are not for the likes of you and me. Cooks Continental Timetable quotes the line under Table 877, but only the section from Tashkent northwest to Moscow can offer any sort of public service. The railway map shows a 2000 mile stretch of line between Novosibirsk and Alma-Ata without a single station. One, however, we must have flown over. It was Karagunda, where the penal camps are not just memories. I would give much to travel that line! From Tashkent a short haul monoplane made a poor substitute for a golden road, but the byways of history along the old silk routes were also a forbidden way, so I had to make do with an air corridor to Samarkand.

The impact of Samarkand is staggering. It speaks to one of Tamerlane and Ulug Beg. I spent my allotted hours amongst its fabulous treasures before shuddering on to the city of Emirs and carpets that is Bukhara. And here you have history breathing down your neck as you wander, deliciously oppressed by ghosts of generations past, along streets unchanged from the dawn of time.

From Bukhara back to Tashkent and the long flight across the time zones of the incredible Kizil Kum and Kara Kum deserts, the swamps of the Murghab River, the ruins of Merv, the oldest of all cities, and the Aral and Caspian Seas until a long-overdue night finally catches up to curtain a mind that is drunk with wonder. But the darkness could not blot out a city sitting squarely on the Volga. The atmosphere in the aircraft was heady with emotion as we passed above the twinkling lights. Few Russians had not lost a son, a husband or a dear friend at Stalingrad and their blood-stained land they loved the more for it.

From Kiev I managed to get back to my beloved railway again, and caught the Danubius Express from Moscow to Bucharest. A steady rain was falling to lay tears on the great black Ukrainian Plain that is also drenched in soldiers' blood and is therefore more terrible. Sad little villages swept by, their houses a contradiction of white paint, their tiny gardens tended almost as gestures of despair.

At Ungeni was the border and the outgoing procedure was no less arduous than that at Brest. For me, in fact, it was worse. An irate personage with the starred epaulettes of an officer bore down upon me in the station while I was changing my remaining roubles into a mixture of western currency. He waved a passport. 'Are you Mr Portway?' he demanded; I was surprised he had to ask. 'Do you realize that your visa is out of order?' His voice was tinged with awe.

I said the last place they promised me an extension was Tashkent.

'*Tashkent*!' he exclaimed. 'Where else have you been?'

I gave him the full list, carefully omitting Vladivostok. I couldn't quite see what the fuss was about.

The officer's face became a darker thunder cloud as each city was reeled off.

'And now Ungeni,' he ended. 'Don't you know your visa was for *Moscow only*?'

'Oh *that*,' I replied gaily, 'Intourist never gave me time to get the thing altered.'

The man all but threw a fit. His voice rose as he recited the laws I had apparently broken.

I said nothing. If I had said anything it would have been rude.

I was to get to know Ungeni rather well. For eighteen hours I was forcibly tethered to its dismal station overlooking an overgrown village. Here my crimes caught up with me, even if they were the wrong crimes. My visa, of course, was the root of the trouble. Vladivostok never came up. Moscow had to be informed of my deficiencies and I suspect that it was poor telephonic communication that was behind much of the delay. I spent a night in a border guards hostel listening to the lullaby of bogie-changing by an infernal machine that lifted coaches bodily into the air for the operation.

There is a myth still going about that the wider 5ft gauge is evidence of traditional Russian suspicion of the outside world. Actually it was an American called Whistler – the one with the mother-in-law – who recommended the wider gauge. The strategic significance is negative, since it is easier for an invader to relay one rail on a broad gauge track than it is to widen the gauge on standard gauge track in the opposite direction. At daybreak I watched the bogie switching operations with some interest. They had the job taped to a fine art and the most numerous articles to be seen on Soviet border stations are discarded bogies.

They gave me the green light that afternoon. A soldier with an automatic rifle escorted me onto the train, gave me an unsmiling salute and waited down the corridor. The train belched and trundled out of the station. Close to the wire marking the frontier it stopped for the customary search for stowaways. As we rolled towards the bridge, at the last moment the soldier jumped off. Having forced me to remain on Soviet soil for eighteen hours they seemed determined to ensure I remained no longer of my own free will. They needn't have worried.